SEP 2016

SORRY
NOT
SORRY

SORRY NOT SORRY

Dreams, Mistakes, and Growing Up

NAYA RIVERA

A TARCHERPERIGEE BOOK

tarcher
perigee

An imprint of Penguin Random House LLC
375 Hudson Street
New York, New York 10014

ISBN 978-0-399-18498-7

Printed in the United States of America
10 9 8 7 6 5 4 3 2 1

Book design by Pauline Neuwirth

Some names and identifying characteristics have been changed to protect the privacy of the individuals involved.

Penguin is committed to publishing works of quality and integrity. In that spirit, we are proud to offer this book to our readers; however, the story, the experiences, and the words are the author's alone.

Wouldn't take nothing for my journey now
—MAYA ANGELOU*

For my family, friends, and my fans

*Because as a wise woman basically once said, "Sorry not sorry"

HELLO, AMERICA (and, hopefully,

other parts of the world):

You might know me from shaking my butt and singing in a cheerleader costume on *Glee*, or from throwing shade (or dodging it) in the tabloids, or maybe even—if you're a super fan or just have a really good memory—from my child-actor days on TV shows like *The Royal Family* or *The Fresh Prince of Bel-Air*.

Which is exactly why I wanted to write this book—I wanted to tell my whole story and talk about the path (which was really more of a roller-coaster ride) that I took to get to be who I am now—an actress, singer, wife, and mother, currently knee-deep in spit-up.

Sometimes growing up happens in the blink of an eyelash extension. You spend years struggling to figure out who you are, and through a lot of those years you feel like it's going to take a bit of divine intervention for you to pull it all together. And then, all of a sudden, you find yourself sitting in the dining room, wondering what to make for dinner and what that baby-related stain on your shirt is, and your adulthood smacks you in the face. And if this hasn't happened to you yet, God willing someday it will. "Holy shit, I did it," you'll think. "I'm a grown-ass woman now." And let me tell you, it will feel good.

Writing this book gave me a chance to relive some of the best and worst times of my life, from predawn wake-up calls as a kindergartener getting ready to shoot my first sitcom to being a twenty-year-old with a fat stack of unpaid bills and an anorexic wallet. But you know what's crazy? Even when I look back at that girl I was decades ago, I still feel like I just saw her yesterday, like she hasn't been gone for all that long.

I started working on this book while I was still shooting *Glee,* and finished the last few chapters with my new baby boy, Josey, sitting in his chair just a few feet away. Motherhood means learning new things and having your expectations turned upside down every single day, but it has also taught me one thing for certain: Josey is my greatest success, and I will never do any better than him.

So yeah, being a mom changes things and makes you feel different in a lot of ways, but for me the big one is this: I'm braver. I've never been afraid of being an open book and telling it like it is, but now I can say, with 100 percent confidence, that zero fucks are given anymore. I don't care what other people think, because being a mom puts everything into perspective. You no longer have to decide what's important to you, because it's right in front of your face, and chances are he's hungry.

Josey gave me wings (I know it's cheesy, but it's true), and with this book I hope to pass on a little bit of that flight to you. Your life doesn't have to be perfect for you to be proud. In fact, I think it's the opposite: the more imperfect your life has been, the prouder you should be, because it means you've come that much further, and also probably had a lot more fun along the way.

And with that—I hope you have as much fun reading this book as I had writing it.

I came into the world ready for the camera—Mom even used my baby book to keep a record of auditions.

1

THE NAY NAY YEARS

FROM THE TIME I was in utero, it was my fate to be in front of the camera. The sound of flashbulbs made me kick, and I'm sure if the sonogram technology had allowed it, you'd have seen little fetus me trying to turn so they got my good side.

My mom was an aspiring actress and model when she unexpectedly got pregnant with me. She was only twenty, but she'd already done pretty well for herself. She had worked a lot for Kohl's in her hometown of Milwaukee, and every weekend there she was in the Sunday paper, modeling a different sweater.

Once she landed in Los Angeles, she ate chicken in a KFC commercial with David Alan Grier and wore bunny ears and danced in a freezer (what?!) in a Smokey Robinson video. In her first trimester, she even made an appearance on *The*

Young and the Restless, where I tried to steal the show by causing a bout of morning sickness that left her making secret trips to the bathroom.

Once I was born, Mom kept it moving and didn't miss a beat. She got me an agent before I could walk, and my grand entrance into life in the public eye was a topless scene: at seven months old I was cast in a Kmart commercial, to crawl across the floor wearing nothing but a diaper.

From baby age on, I booked print ads, almost all of which were shot in front of a gray seamless, with me wearing a floral romper, OshKosh, or Plum Pudding—the height of late eighties, early nineties kids' fashion. Even as a tot model, though, I couldn't just stand there, nor was it all fun. It was work! I'd have to do stuff like hula-hoop, blow bubbles, pretend to laugh, or (the worst) hold hands with other kids— usually their hands were sweaty and clammy, or they'd pick their nose right up to the very last second, then reach their fingers toward mine.

Even though I'd just recently stopped wearing diapers, I was three feet tall and all business. I got the hang of modeling really quickly and easily took direction from the photographer. When other models would get all teary eyed and hiccupy about holding hands with someone they didn't know, I was always annoyed. "Why do we have to convince you?" I'd think. "Just do your job and hold my damn hand and take the picture!" I didn't even pick my nose.

I also started to book television commercials, and soon I was Mattel's go-to ethnic girl, doing ads for Cabbage Patch dolls or twirling around with a Bubble Angel Barbie.

Sometimes all they wanted in the shot was my brown hand, so I'd get a manicure and then have to hold a toy very, very still while the cameras got their shot.

My agent was a woman named Arletta Proch, who repped mostly babies and child actors. My mom had a pager so Arletta could get a hold of us when we were out running

NAYA RIVERA

PHOTOGRAPH BY COLLEEN CLER

around for auditions, and when the pager would start buzzing, we always knew I'd gotten a job. We'd head straight to a pay phone, and Mom would call into the agency. They'd celebrate by clanging a cowbell on their end, and on our end Mom would pick me up so I could reach the receiver, and I'd scream as loud as I could into the phone. No matter if we were at a shopping mall in the Valley or at a phone booth in the middle of Hollywood Boulevard, I practically tore my lungs out, screaming bloody murder, to show how excited I was. In retrospect, it's amazing my mother didn't get picked up on suspicion of kidnapping.

At the time, my dad had a full-time job working in IT, which gave my mom the opportunity to devote herself full time to my career, and she founded a company called One-Plus-One Management. She was my manager, and I her only client (my husband and I joke now that we're going to bring it back, and that I'll represent him under One-Plus-One Management).

Make no mistake, though: Mom was no mere momager. She was a badass, and really good at her job. She took my auditions very seriously and considered every detail when helping me look the part. We made a lot of trips to T.J.Maxx, where we'd dig through the racks until my mom found exactly what I needed. She also invested in makeup and props. I had a mole on my chin that we'd sometimes cover up using this thick, creamy makeup that was invented for burn victims to use to cover scars (to this day, I still use it for contouring), and we got really expensive flippers made—fake teeth that we could plug in when a real one fell out.

If I was auditioning to play a girl who was kind of nerdy and wore her hair in braids, you could bet I'd show up with fake glasses, braids, and some dork-ass outfit of clashing plaids and prints. Since I was mixed race, I could play a lot of different ethnicities, from just plain old dark-skinned white girl to Latino to African American. Mom stopped short of giving me a spray tan, but if I was auditioning for a role specifically for a black girl, you could bet she'd encourage me to play outside in the sun.

Mom's diligence (and my hard work, of course) paid off, and at age five I landed my first television role on CBS's *The Royal Family*. I honestly don't remember the audition, but when I heard that I got it, I bet you could hear me scream all the way in San Diego.

Created and executive-produced by Eddie Murphy, the show was a family comedy that starred Redd Foxx and Della Reese as a retired couple who are forced to deal when their daughter and three grandchildren move in with them.

I played the youngest grandchild, Hillary, and Redd Foxx and I were intergenerational BFFs from the moment we met. He started to tell people that I really was his granddaughter, and I believed him. He and his wife were so nice to my whole family; they were always bringing me souvenirs from their trips, like a floral lei from Hawaii, or a tiny ceramic red fox—get it?

Redd had a reputation for being a flashy dresser—he believed in dressing like a king—and so he got a lot of his clothes custom made to fit his opulent tastes. When he'd hit upon an outfit he really liked, he'd tell his tailor, "Get baby girl one too," and then, boom! we'd be matching—which is how Redd and I ended up going on *The Arsenio Hall Show* looking like we'd both just raided Michael Jackson's closet.

In 2013, I went on *Arsenio* again, to talk about *Glee*, and he surprised me with the footage from twenty-two years earlier. In it Redd is wearing a red (again, get it? the man liked to work a theme) jacket covered in gold chains and tassels, a red beret, and giant sunglasses. I'm wearing a cream-colored two-piece suit, also covered in gold chains and tassels, with a giant crown on the back. Arsenio asks me if I want to be a model, and without missing a beat, I tell him I'm not into it because "I already did that!" Then he asks if I want to get married someday. My answer? "No!"—said in a tone of voice that implied that my prekindergarten self had never heard such a stupid question.

However, my favorite outfit that Redd gave me, and possibly my favorite outfit of all time, never made a television appearance. It was a gold-lamé bandeau top that showed a little belly; a giant gold, poufed skirt, with a black net tutu underneath; and a gold biker hat.

Once, I came downstairs with the whole ensemble on, determined to wear it to preschool. "Mom," I said, twirling around, "this is so cool. People need to see this!" Mom rightly figured that it might be a little much for me to go to preschool dressed like a baby Paula Abdul, and marched me right back upstairs to change.

That outfit is still in a box in my closet, though. The bandeau now barely fits around my foot, which is sad because I would definitely still rock that look if I could.

On *The Royal Family*, I fell in love with being on TV. I'd just started preschool not too long before, so I didn't really have much old life to compare my new life to, but I was still aware that I was doing something special. We'd wake up for call times at four thirty in the morning, and quietly tiptoe around and out the door so we wouldn't wake up my dad before he had to get up and go to work. I never once complained about having to get out of bed so early, because secretly I knew that if I was up before the sun, I must be important.

The schedule for being on a half-hour, multicamera sitcom was super regimented but not terribly strenuous. We were finished each day by the middle of the afternoon and didn't ever have to shoot on weekends.

Every Monday started with a table read of that week's script. I still couldn't read, so I was basically a parrot in pigtails. Mom would sit me on her lap and read lines off the blue-paper script, over my shoulder. When it would come to my lines, she'd say them out loud and I'd repeat them back. This was usually the first time the cast would see the script, so there was always a lot of laughing and joking about the lines.

Tuesdays and Wednesdays were for the blocking rehearsals we needed before shooting in front of a live studio audience, which is a lot like live theater. They use terms like "downstage" and "upstage," and you have to learn to cheat yourself, which means keeping your body open to the camera and the audience no matter what you're doing.

When the script called for me to do physical comedy—like running into the room while shooting Redd with a water gun, or making a giant mess by inexplicably pouring buckets of paint into a birdbath—I had to learn how to do it without ever turning my back toward the camera.

I remember one particular scene where I had to pretend I needed to pee really bad while they slowly unspooled me from a sarong. Another episode called for me to sing a song and do a little dance, hitting three different marks along the way as I walked off camera. I shot this scene with a 102-degree fever—not because anyone told me I had to but because I insisted. There was no way I was missing a day of work or a fun scene! And even though I was burning up, I nailed it.

On Thursdays we'd shoot any scenes that were too long to do in front of an audience, and then Friday was the big payoff. Shooting in front of a live audience on a Friday night always feels like a party, especially when you're only five. When the actors come in, you do a precurtain call, where you run on set and are introduced to the audience. The adults would crack jokes, take bows, and shake hands with the audience, but since I was just a little kid, all I did was wave. Since we filmed at night, my dad was able to come when he got off work, and it always made me smile when he cheered extra loud.

Sometimes people would bring presents or flowers after the taping, and after a few episodes of the show had aired, I started to get fan mail. My mom and I would sit in my dressing room with a stack of little headshot cards. She would open the letters, read them to me, and then I'd sign the card, in my child's handwriting, with a little heart and "Naya," and then we'd send it back. To this day, I still draw a little heart when I sign my name—which actually irks me, because I think it looks childish, but I can't help it because it's totally automatic at this point.

I remember one time my mom opened a letter and started to read it to me. "Okay," she said, "make it out to 'Eddie.'" She started to spell it out for me, then stopped. "Oh no," she said, "Eddie's . . . in jail? How does he even watch TV?" Needless to say, Eddie and I would not go on to become pen pals.

The Royal Family wasn't a kids' show, so I didn't have many fans in my peer group, but occasionally people would see us out in public and come up to my parents to tell them how much they liked the show. One such person was Tupac, who saw us in LAX and came over to introduce himself to my mom.

The story goes that he picked me up and held me for several minutes while he and my mom—who can chat up anyone—hit it off. Where are the photos of this, Mom and Dad?! Seriously, why didn't you take pictures? Le sigh . . . But still: Tupac held me. Legendary.

On set, the cast and crew really were like a family. Every Thursday, Redd's friend Bubba would make gumbo for everyone, and on the days when my mom wasn't eating gumbo, she was talking about how good it had been or how good it was gonna be. I was a weirdo kid who loved shrimp, so I gobbled it up right along with her.

Redd Foxx was most well-known for his role on *Sanford and Son*, a show that had been created by legendary television producer Norman Lear and was hailed as having paved the way for African American sitcoms. Redd was first and foremost a comedian, and as the title character, Fred Sanford, he had a bit about having a heart attack. He'd clutch his chest dramatically and wail and moan about, warning his wife that he was coming up to see her. It was all part of his schtick.

On October 11, 1991—less than a month after *The Royal Family* had premiered—Redd and I were running our lines on set. He was sitting in an easy chair, and I was standing on my mark in front of him, when all of a sudden he kind of slumped over and fell to the floor. For a while, no one moved. One of the producers even yelled, "Redd, come on!" Everyone assumed it was just part of his routine, so we waited patiently for him to stand back up. Except, he didn't.

Della Reese, who played his wife, was the first to figure out that something really was happening. She rushed over, leaned down to him, and heard him saying, "Get my wife—get my wife." Della stood up and started screaming, which jolted everyone in the room into action. The assistant director yelled for someone to get an ambulance, and my mom, who had been sitting and watching rehearsals with Redd's wife, tried desperately to calm her down and assure her that everything was going to be okay.

I didn't move, though. I'd been taught to stay on my mark, so that's what I did. My dad happened to be on set that day. Finally, he noticed that I was still standing there like a statue, so he ran over and scooped me up. He and my mom took me up to my dressing room, where they set me down with some coloring books and instructions not to move—again—while they went back downstairs and tried to help.

I hadn't really known my own grandparents, so for all intents and purposes Redd was my grandpa. I was way too young to process it at the time, but now, when I look back, I realize how special and unique it was for the cast of a TV show to have such offscreen camaraderie and genuine love. The whole cast and crew followed Redd's ambulance to the hospital, and we sat there, his TV family and his real family, all mixed together in the waiting room, praying and trying to comfort one another. When the doctor came out to tell us that Redd had passed, he delivered the news to the entire group.

As you can imagine, everyone took it really hard. Redd was such a presence wherever he went. He'd started his career in stand-up, and he was one of those people who could turn anything into a stage and anyone into an audience. He was the first person I knew who died, and I still remember his funeral—which was held in Las Vegas—very vividly. It was open casket. He looked very kingly in a white suit, and it was a fitting tribute to a man who liked to live large.

Della sang "What a Wonderful World," a song that can make me teary eyed to this day. My mom had become especially close to Redd and his wife, Ka, so she took it really hard. She'd bring me to visit Redd's grave, where Ka would give me a cigar (one of Redd's favorite things) and tell me I could give Redd a present. We'd dig a little hole, stick the cigar in it, and then she would light it. We'd watch the smoke curl up and into the air, and in my five-year-old brain I imagined him six feet underground, smoking away in that white suit and being just the same as he always was.

After Redd passed, the producers briefly brought in Jackée to play Della's sister and try to keep the show going, but as my mom said, it just wasn't the same without Redd. *The Royal Family* came to an end after just one season.

Glee would eventually be filmed on the same Paramount lot where we shot *The Royal Family*, and every day, on my way to the set, I'd walk past the day care where my mom would drop off my baby brother before she and I would head to work. I love the Paramount lot, and returning to work there so many years later felt like a homecoming. It made me think about my TV beginnings, and Redd, a lot. He was one of the first people to really believe in me, and I've always wanted to make him proud. Someday I'm gonna take that fox and a Ouija board over to Stage 16 and see if I can say hello. I'd love to tell him what I'm up to, and make sure he knows how much I loved that gold-lamé bandeau top.

SLAYING IT IN THE EARLY NINETIES

At this point in my life, I didn't know that much about school, but I knew that I liked acting better. I was around adults all the time, I was getting attention (see above, re Tupac), and I got to wear fancy clothes and do silly things that would have gotten me in trouble had I tried to do them at home.

After *The Royal Family* was canceled and I wasn't going to an on-set tutor anymore, my parents enrolled me in the local public elementary school. At night, after I finished my home-

work, my mom would make me get my lines for whatever audition I had coming up and go into her room. When I was
super little, Mom would just repeat everything over and over,
and have me repeat it back to her. Even once I could read,
though, she still made me go off book every time I went into
a casting. This meant I couldn't walk in a room and read my
lines from a piece of paper, even if that's what everyone else
was doing; I had to memorize them. To this day, I can still
learn my lines super fast, and can recall conversations I had
months ago nearly verbatim (my poor husband, right?).

For the first sixteen years of my life, my mom was the only
acting coach I had. She was damn good at it too. She'd give
me pointers on delivery and body language, like, "Okay, but
next time put your hand on your hip when you say that
word," or she'd demonstrate the facial expressions to make
when I was supposed to get people to laugh, or when I was
supposed to look mad or unhappy.

In a lot of ways, my mom and I had a very adult relationship, but at the core I was still a kid. Sometimes our nightly
sessions of running lines would end in a screaming match,
with me crying because I just wanted to play, or frustrated
because I didn't think she was listening to me. I also hated
some auditions, especially those kid cattle calls for commercials that involved several hours of standing in line.

Eventually I got savvy enough to bargain when I knew that
an audition would be particularly annoying, which was how I
ended up with an all-white bunny named Duchess. Ah,
Duchess—I was super into her for, like, the first two days, then
totally forgot about her. Eventually her tiny bunny water bot-

tle proved to be no match for a summer day in Valencia, and she succumbed to heatstroke. After Duchess, Mom wised up, and my rewards were only of the inanimate variety.

The first thing I booked after *The Royal Family* was a guest spot on *The Fresh Prince of Bel-Air*. While I hated commercial auditions, I took television auditions very seriously. I remember that I was barely out of that casting when I burst into tears. I was convinced that I'd done a horrible job and wasn't going to get it.

Then we got a page from Arletta, and I went from midmeltdown to screaming with joy into a pay phone. The role I landed was only for one episode, and one scene, which wasn't even with Will Smith, but I was on set long enough for him to call me cute.

My mom and I were sitting on some stairs, rehearsing my lines, and were (unintentionally!!) blocking the entrance to his dressing room. He came by and asked us to move but also introduced himself and called me pretty.

I beamed. "Wow, Mom! That's the Fresh Prince!"

So yeah—Tupac *and* Will Smith? I was totally slaying in the early nineties.

After this, I booked a recurring role on *Family Matters*. I have to be honest—I think this was when I reached my prime in terms of my physical appearance. I played Gwendolyn, who was the seven-year-old love interest of Little Richie, and the costume department really knew what it was doing. Gwendolyn had the best hair and the best outfits! Her hair was always half-up/half-down and full of scrunchies. Each of her outfits was made up of at least seventeen articles of clothing—it was all about the layers. She'd be in leggings under a skirt with a long-sleeved shirt under a short-sleeved shirt with a bandanna around her neck, and then they'd top it all off with something like a pair of little yellow socks and red Chuck Taylors.

On a Valentine's Day episode, they paired a red dress with a leopard-print coat and a big red flower in my hair—the look beats any red-carpet ensemble I've worn to this day. Another highlight was when I got to drive a battery-powered Barbie Jeep. This made a *huge* impression on me. I thought it was the coolest thing ever, and I loved it so much that it (unfortunately) influenced my taste in real cars when I finally got my driver's license more than ten years later.

Richie wasn't just my on-screen love; offscreen I was convinced I was going to marry him. He could dance and he had the best Jheri curl on TV—what more could a girl want?

I thought he looked like Michael Jackson, and I was obsessed. I'd call his house to talk to him, and Richie and I would tie up the phone lines for hours. As to what our conversations were actually about? Beats me. The pinnacle of our romance was the *Family Matters* wrap party. As all the adults were getting drunk, and the older kids were being cool, Richie and I burned up the dance floor until we were sweaty—him with his Michael Jackson moves and me with the running man, which I had mastered so well that it should've been in the special-skills section of my résumé.

Alas—sometimes young love is just not meant to last, and I have no idea where Richie is these days. Nor, if I'm being honest, can I even remember his real name.

My on-screen roles definitely led to some offscreen perks. Michael Jackson's niece was also an actor, and we were on several auditions together. Over time, our moms became friends, enough so that I was invited to her birthday party at Neverland Ranch. I was still too young to really understand what was so special about it, but my mom was freaking out—even though she wasn't allowed to come with me (the girl's mom assured us that there were chaperones, and that Michael was not one of them).

The day of the party, we all met at a central location, where we would be taken to the ranch. Everyone else on the bus was like twelve or thirteen, but I was a freaking baby—small enough that I was still wearing white tights! Nicole Richie was one of the other kids on the bus, and when she saw a five-year-old climb on board by herself, Nicole and her friend took me under their wing and let me sit with them. The bus ride was so long that I got sleepy and laid down and took a nap in Nicole's lap. When I woke up, I saw that I'd drooled all over her leg.

Once we were at Neverland, we rode the rides and watched a movie in a full-size theater. I remember walking up to a concession stand that was filled with popcorn and candy. I had planned on just drooling at the snacks from behind the glass because I didn't have any money, but then the guy working the counter said, "Do you want anything? Everything is free here." If this had been a movie, we would have cut to a trippy echo sequence at that moment: "Everything is free . . . Everything is free . . ." I'd never heard anything so glorious in my brief little life. I gobbled up Sour

Patch Kids and Raisinets and Twizzlers, and then stayed awake for the entire bus ride home, all hopped up on sugar.

THE FIRST ETHNIC DOROTHY (AT MY ELEMENTARY SCHOOL, AT LEAST)

I booked one of the most important roles of my career, far away from Hollywood, when I played Dorothy in *The Wizard of Oz*. No, not on Broadway, but even better: at Valencia Valley Elementary School. The school put on *The Wizard of Oz* every year, and the teacher in charge was this biggish woman who always wore oversize muumuus and had long gray hair. During story time, she'd make kids rub her bunions. I was totally disgusted by it at the time, and now that I look back on it, I wonder—how did this bitch not get fired?

But that's an aside: *The Wizard of Oz* was her passion, and she was obsessed with making it as good as it could be. The year that I could audition, she was practically salivating at the chance to have a professional actress in the lead role.

She went through the dog and pony show of holding auditions, but I knew I was going to get it—hello, I had credits! I was such a little monster back then that I'm surprised I didn't walk in and hand her my résumé. Afterward, I stood in a circle of girls who had tried out for the part and put on a show of asking everyone who they thought was going to get it. Even at the time, I knew that was bratty behavior—but did it anyway.

Diva antics aside, the show was a hit—in the video you can see me hitting every mark and making sure I enunciate every line. My parents were just as proud then as they were when I landed a role on national television—my mom even stayed up the night before, covering my shoes with gold glitter and red spray paint.

The Wizard of Oz was definitely the highlight of my elementary school years. Even though I was still just in the single digits, it was pretty obvious that school and I were not destined to get along. I got suspended twice before I even made it to fifth grade.

My family moved a lot, and in total I went to three different elementary schools. I was never nervous about being the new kid, though, and always had a pretty easy time making friends. In second grade, I met my friend Madison, who is still my best friend to this day. Other friendships didn't have quite the same staying power.

In fourth grade, I befriended this girl Sarah who was a total tomboy and kind of a bully. One day she decided to spin me around by my hair. I screamed and screamed for her to stop, trying to keep up before she ripped my ponytail completely off my head. When she wouldn't stop, I resorted to more drastic measures and bit the hell out of her arm. It was a little bit of real-life foreshadowing of the *Glee* episode where Santana gets her ass kicked by Lauren and resorts to biting. That aside—somehow I got suspended, and that bitch Sarah got off scot-free, even though she'd started it!

Unlike the creepy bunion teacher, not every teacher at the schools I attended was stoked about having an actress in their midst. At one school, it was clear from day one that the principal had it out for me and didn't consider acting a worthwhile pursuit. My parents were constantly fighting with the school to get it to recognize my on-set tutor hours, and you could see the look of disdain on the principal's face every time my mom would try to talk to her about how I was going to miss a few more days of school because of shooting. Like anyone learns anything in elementary school anyway.

One day I was sitting in class, minding my own business, when I was suddenly called into the principal's office.

"Naya," she said, with all the seriousness of a counterterrorism agent interrogating a member of ISIS. "Do you recognize this note?" She slid a piece of paper across the table, and, sure enough, I did recognize it. It was a note I'd written to my friend Kate about a boy in our class. "Johnny smells so bad," I'd scrawled in pencil across a piece of wide-ruled paper. "Sometimes I want him to die."

When I nodded, she sat back smugly in her chair. "This," she said, "is a very serious matter."

She called in my mom and announced that I was getting suspended yet again, but this time for making a death threat against a fellow student!

My mom is not the kind of woman to take anything lying down, but I think at this point she'd had enough of this school and decided she wasn't wasting any more time on this woman than she already had.

She just shrugged, told me to gather up my stuff, and we went home. It was the one time in my life that I didn't get in trouble with my parents for getting in trouble at school. Instead, I played in the park, watched tons of Nickelodeon, and had a pretty nice little vacation.

Even as a child, I knew that acting was a job, and I liked that feeling of responsibility. I liked to work hard and felt fulfilled knowing that I was good at something. Sometimes this work ethic leaked into other areas of my life. I was competitive and didn't just play—I couldn't understand how other kids could do something and not try their absolute best. For example, between the ages of six and ten, I was an absolute beast when it came to handball. How this became my passion du jour, I have no idea, but I practiced at home so I could dominate the playground handball scene at recess. I was the champ of the court, and I got real mean when other people didn't take it as seriously as I did.

In my grade there was this one girl, Melissa, who was rumored to have been a crack baby or something, and she had a deformed hand. When we played handball, we turned into a bunch of trash-talking seven-year-olds, and Melissa made the mistake of calling me poor.

I turned around and yelled, "Oh yeah?! Why are you playing handball, anyway, when you only have one hand?!" Then I went right back to whacking the shit outta that ball. I later apologized to Melissa, because as soon as I walked off the court, the other kids were like, "Yo, Naya, that's messed up," and as the sweat dried off my forehead, I had to admit that, yes, it was really fucked up. So lesson learned: not all is fair in the name of love and handball.

BEING A CHILD ACTOR—AND LIVING TO TELL THE TALE

The Royal Family only lasted one season, but I really believe that it had all the elements of a great sitcom and could have been as successful as *The Fresh Prince of Bel-Air* or *Family Matters* if Redd hadn't passed away.

When this happened, my family obviously mourned Redd's death, but we also mourned the passing of the show. That kind of opportunity doesn't come along very often, and when I was cast on the show, we saw it as the beginning of a long career—it was tough to watch it kind of sputter to a halt less than a year later. I could have been the Tatyana Ali of my day, and picking up residuals forever.

In retrospect, though, I think that everything happened for me with my career at the perfect time. If I'd been a successful kid actor, I'd probably be way more crazy than I am now, and doing fucked-up things with those residual checks!

I think it's hard for child actors to make the transition to adulthood (on-screen and offscreen), because they have everything they want at such an early age. You get tons of attention and people are always telling you how great you are, not to mention all the material perks. Even though you're a little kid, people turn you into the boss. This happens especially when the kid becomes the breadwinner in the family, and I think that is hard for the kids and the parents—how are you going to discipline a kid when they're the one making all the money?

Also, when you're super successful as a little kid, you're not mentally developed enough to understand that things could change at any time. You just think your life is always going to be this cool—then, all of a sudden, you hit that awkward stage in life, your roles start to dry up, and you're back to being a normal kid even though you're totally unprepared for normalcy.

Even if you still manage to keep it somewhat together, you're always going to struggle to get casting directors and audiences to see you as anything other than that kid from that thing (see Haley Joel Osment or Jonathan Lipnicki). I find the Olsen twins incredibly impressive, because they somehow managed to make the switch from cute kids to cool adults without losing their minds, but I also think it's no surprise that they decided to focus on something other than acting. Sometimes I get annoyed when people assume I was just starting out when I was on *Glee*—when I've really been working since I was five—but on the whole I'm really thankful that I got to have several years of low-key, behind-the-scenes training.

As frustrating as it is not to get what you want right away, success is a lot sweeter when it's a slow build. You want to always be getting better, and to be moving on to bigger opportunities. You want to be looking forward, not looking back wistfully at how you had everything you'd ever wanted at age six. Who wants to peak as a kid, as a teenager, or even in their early twenties? Then it's all downhill for the next six decades, and that's just—well, yikes!

I plan to live a long time, and I want each stage of my life to get progressively more fancy. If it's all uphill from here, and I've still got some work to put in, then that's fine by me. I prefer it that way.

SORRY:

- *Making fun of an alleged crack baby on the playground. Wherever you are, Melissa, I am so sorry about that.*

- *Male prisoners writing fan letters to a five-year-old. Oof . . . just creepy.*

- *Missed photo ops with super hot legendary rappers (though this sorry mostly falls on my parents).*

- *Drooling on Nicole Richie's knee (sorry, girl).*

- *Redd Foxx's premature death and losing such a talented comedian, a warm person, and a loving surrogate grandpa.*

NOT SORRY:

- *Getting introduced to my passion—acting—while still in preschool and knowing even then that it was what I wanted to do for the rest of my life.*

- *Learning to memorize lines before I even learned to spell (an invaluable skill that's stuck with me).*

▪ *All the outfits Redd got me (can't go wrong with head-to-toe gold) and all the outfits I got to wear on Family Matters.*

▪ *That Barbie Jeep, though . . .*

▪ *That I didn't become a famous child actor or peak at age nine.*

I AM MY OWN AFTER-SCHOOL SPECIAL
Learning to Love the Skin I'm In

THINK BACK TO yourself as a preteen. Puberty hasn't hit yet, but it's starting to peek around the corner, so you're all kinds of awkward. Braces. Training bras that are flat fabric on an even flatter chest. Hairy legs. Weird growth spurts that leave some parts of your body longer than they should be and others shorter. Nothing about you is proportionate. Nothing is cute.

These awkward years smacked the shit out of me. I hated my quarter-white, quarter-black, half–Puerto Rican, and all-frizz hair. And my boobs weren't even boobs; they were just big nipples. All the girls I knew at school were starting to wear bras, but when I asked my mom to take me shopping for one, she—oh lady of complete and total bluntness—just looked me up and down and asked, "What for?"

By the end of elementary school, my acting career had totally dried up. At that age you're too old to play a cute kid, too young to play a hot teenager, and basically no one wants you. Everything is made even weirder by the fact that you know so many people. I'd go in and audition for the same casting directors who'd once gushed over me as a five-year-old, and I could practically see them grimace, like, "Woof! it's unfortunate how this one turned out . . ."

I was still giving it a shot, though, and taking vocal lessons to try and keep myself good and ready should that big break suddenly materialize. My teacher was an old standards singer, and she taught me Billie Holiday jazz tunes and classic Broadway numbers. They were huge songs with tons of runs and show-stopping high notes, but way too big for a kid, which is why I developed vocal nodules at the age of ten. I'd been overexerting myself and basically screaming to hit these notes, and the result was that I had to go on serious vocal rest (and fire my singing teacher).

I had a complete sobbing breakdown in the car upon hearing the news. I thought my voice was going to be gone forever. "I'm never gonna sing again!"

"Shh, Naya, shh!" my mom said, trying both to calm me down and keep me quiet. It also didn't help that I was a big recess screamer, yelling bloody murder for no good reason as I ran around the playground. For the next several weeks, I had to avoid talking as much as possible and would catch myself during heated games of handball—when I'd score and turn around triumphantly, ready to talk some shit, only to remember my vocal rest and realize that shit-talking isn't nearly as impressive when you have to whisper it.

It also didn't help that my parents' marriage was still rocky—just the year before, my dad had had an affair while my mom was pregnant with my sister. She kicked him out, and I remember going to visit him at his apartment, which was your stereotypical sad-dad bachelor pad: dirty beige carpet that no amount of shampooing can clean, a futon as a bed, and just enough dishware to heat up a burrito. I was like, "Dad, this is gross. You need to go home."

Meanwhile my mom and her pregnancy hormones weren't faring much better. She was a devotee of the scorned-lady playlist, always crying in her room to some Anita Baker or Toni Braxton. "Mom," I said, "talk to Dad."

The next time I saw my dad, I said, "Dad, talk to Mom!" Finally, they hired a babysitter to watch my brother and me, and when we came home, they were sitting together at the kitchen table. Mom turned to us and said, "Your father's moving back in." Woo-hoo!

Shortly thereafter, Dad got a new job and we moved out of our cute, but tiny, house and into a big new one. I got my own room with one of those amazing window seats where the cushion lifts up so that you can hide (or just store) stuff in there, and I got to pick out a decorating scheme. Pink and white, bitches!

But a new house didn't solve the family problems—far from it—and I just felt anxious all the time. I missed working and the sense of routine and purpose that came with it. I also just straight-up loved acting, and although a part of me knew that the reasons I wasn't getting roles were out of my control, a bigger part of me took it as a sign that there was something wrong with me. I felt lost and didn't know what to do with myself. I went into junior high feeling like a loser and a has-been. I didn't want to come home after school and watch TV; I wanted to be on TV.

One day I just decided to see how long I could go without eating. I never thought I was fat—if anything, my lack of boobs and scrawny legs told me that I was actually too skinny—but being extra-OCD about food soon became my thing. It gave me something to think about all day, and it was a secret that I could obsess over without anyone else knowing about it.

I just avoided food at all costs. If my mom had packed a lunch for me, I'd either trash it or find some excuse to give it away. If she'd given me money to buy my lunch, I just didn't use it and would save it for the weekends. My eating habits— or total lack thereof—didn't really stand out at school, since it seemed like everyone I sat with at lunch was also on her own weird food trip. My best friend, Madison, was able to convince her mom to buy her SlimFast bars, and there were other girls in my grade who cranked through a six pack of Diet Coke in a day, all while nibbling on the same bag of pretzels.

In my own sick and twisted way, I'd look at those girls who were sort of dieting and feel superior. Because you want to know how to really lose weight? Just don't eat *anything. Ever.*

All through my years of working and auditions, no one had ever even called me chubby, so my budding anorexia had nothing to do with work—I just hated everything about myself. My mom worried that I'd catch a cold when I left for school in the morning—in California!—because my hair was still wet and dripping with gel in a desperate attempt to keep it from curling itself into a mushroom cloud. I also had a mole on my chin that made me feel like a haggard old witch, and I got teased nonstop about it. "Naya's so gross with that mole on her chin. I wonder if hair grows out of it?" people would say loudly enough for me to hear.

I knew that I wasn't one of the prettiest or the most popular girls in school. I wasn't a total outcast—all the popular kids gathered in the quad at lunch or between classes, and I could hang out there too if I wanted, but I knew I wasn't going to win the crown at any school dances. I couldn't work my way into being the prettiest girl in school, but my level of popularity seemed like something that I could control, so soon I was splitting my time between not eating and trying to up my social status.

Every day I'd scheme on it. I'd come home from school, do my homework, bluff my way through dinner, and then sit down to decompress and pick apart my day. I had this blue spiral-bound notebook that I'd gotten from the Ross Dress for Less discount department store. The cover had a moon on it, with "journal" printed across the front in silver script. In it, I'd write things like:

Dear Diary,

Today sucked. This is why:

1. My outfit wasn't on point. My T-shirt was too big and didn't fit right, my shoes looked dirty, and my mom still won't let me stuff the tongues with socks.

2. My hair looked wet in the morning but was a frizz fest by the time I got to geography. Don't use *Bed Head After Party* anymore. Go back to *Pink Oil Moisturizer*. It's supposed to last all day.

3. Cindy's mad at me because I can't spend the night this weekend. Hopefully she'll still let me borrow her *Chronic 2* album. Mom won't let me buy it, and I love that song "Can't Make a Ho a Housewife."

4. Why don't I have a pager? Everyone else has a pager. I MUST get a pager.

5. Study for math tests! Mr. Johnson announces grades when he hands papers back, and now everyone knows I got a D.

6. Eat fewer crackers. Today I had five. Four tomorrow MAX.

7. Talk to everyone in the quad. Even if I don't really like them.

8. Get more butterfly clips.

Tomorrow will be better.

xo,
Naya

I'd emerge from a good journaling session with a clear sense of purpose and a list of demands that usually seemed completely unreasonable and out of left field to my parents.

"Dad," I'd scream as I emerged from my bedroom, "can you take me to get a yellow shirt? I need a yellow shirt!" Nine times out of ten, they'd flat-out refuse, so I'd head back to the journal to figure out a plan B.

The junior high I went to made us wear uniforms, so I didn't have much to work with in the wardrobe department, but all the finesse—and signifiers of your clique—was in how you styled it. My style icon was Brittany, the coolest girl in school. Our uniforms were made up of a rather dumpy pair of khaki shorts that came down almost to our knee caps and a giant, thick white-cotton polo or T-shirt with sleeves that hung down to our elbows.

Brittany, however, was totally unrestrained by these two horrible articles of clothing. She would take the T-shirt and roll the sleeves all the way up to her shoulders, then tie them together across the back with a piece of gift-wrapping ribbon, even curling the ends so they hung down between her shoulder blades in spirals.

Then, she'd take her shorts and roll them up so high that you could practically see her underwear. Really, it looked like she was wearing a giant diaper and had just taken a shit in her pants. However, everyone was super into it, so I was, like, well, obviously I gotta do that.

But my legs were so skinny that it looked like I was walking around in a pair of XXL Depends, not a super cool

Brittany diaper, so, ugh! File that under just another popularity plan that backfired. I was also always shooting myself in the foot by getting can duty at lunch.

Can duty was basically the junior high chain gang, and our school's version of detention. If you were late to classes, got caught passing notes, or back-talked to a teacher, you were assigned to spend your entire lunch period going around the school grounds and picking up cans. What was worse, to ensure that you really did it, you had to collect at least fifty cans each time. And trust me—even if my hair looked good that day, and I'd rolled up my sleeves and tied them with the absolute coolest glittery pink ribbon in all of Valencia—no one was going to want to talk to me while I was digging through the trash in search of Dr Pepper cans.

I convinced my dad to help me out by raiding the recycling at his office, so for the entirety of my eighth-grade year, he was driving around with a bunch of garbage in the backseat of his car so I could turn in my requisite cans and still have time to glad-hand my way through lunch hour. Ah, the sacrifices that parents make for their children!

Finally, eighth-grade graduation rolled around, and as a celebration, my mom let me do two things that had previously been banned in the Rivera household: shave my legs and straighten my hair.

Or, to be more precise, my mom did both. For me. The day of our graduation ceremony, convinced that I'd nick the hell out of my knees and bleed to death, she had me sit on the side of the bathtub and lathered up my legs—only from the knee down, of course—and did the shaving for me, with a

Shaved legs, straight hair, ready to take on the world. Maybe.

little pink-plastic disposable razor. I also got a new outfit, a little orange two-piece with matching sequined top and bottom, and walked across that stage feeling like I was on top of the world. I had straight hair and smooth legs. What the hell could go wrong?

HIGH SCHOOL HELL

At first it seemed that high school was going to live up to my mile-high expectations. My best friend, Madison, had a boyfriend, and all around me everybody was getting boyfriends. Inevitably, "Get a boyfriend" was soon added to my nightly to-do lists, and it became my mission. As I'd walk down the halls in between classes, I'd scan the boys' passing faces. Who was going to be my boyfriend?

Soon, I had a target. Stewart would be my boyfriend. Stewart and I had barely talked, and I knew practically nothing about him, except that he was half-white, half-black—mixed race just like me. So, duh, obviously this was going to work. Stewart and I could do this. We started to exchange a few more words here and there—he'd come up to my locker during passing period and ask for a piece of gum, and I would give it to him. Then one day Madison and I walked past him and his friend Alex as we were leaving the quad.

"Hey, Naya," Alex yelled. "He wants you to be his girlfriend." Stewart just stood there.

"Okay," I yelled back, and it was Alex who flashed us a thumbs-up. Still, though—success! I had a boyfriend!

The next day, I walked up to Stewart and got his phone number, figuring that if we were going to be in a relationship, then we'd better start talking on the phone. Because that's what boyfriends and girlfriends did in ninth grade—talked on the phone. A lot.

Except Stewart didn't have much to say. Forget that—Stewart didn't have anything to say. I had wanted it to last, but, alas, Stewart just didn't seem to be the one, so the next day I told Alex to tell him that I was dumping him. Alex seemed totally up to the task, and asked no questions. Madison couldn't believe that I'd broken up with Stewart, but I felt confident in my decision, since I now knew that having a boyfriend wasn't really all it was cracked up to be. I was also certain that I knew what key qualities my future true love would have:

HE HAS TO BE . . .

- successful in some career or working toward it

- financially well off, and able to spoil me rotten

- driving a nice car — no POSs!

- handsome, possibly male model material, preferably with long hair

- sexy

- funny! has to be able to laugh with me (not @ me)

- creative — i.e., music, art, etc.

- sensitive but not gay
- romantic but not corny
- a good kisser
- good in bed
- good @ kissing my ass
- able to cook (because I can't)
- able to clean (+ not bitch @ me for it)
- able to travel (with me)
- spontaneous!
- responsible
- at the same spiritual level as me (wherever I am @ that time)
- nice to the family
- able to go out to dinner a lot
- able to afford several trips to Rodeo Drive
- nice
- patient (especially w/ me)
- all or mostly all of these things

Even though I'd changed schools and my love life was looking up, I still wasn't eating. I'd always been thin, but now I was in skin-and-bones territory. In junior high, when we'd lived in an apartment complex, I'd sneak down to the gym and spend hours on the elliptical machines to burn off the few calories that I'd consumed that day. Now that we were in our own house, I'd do yoga videos in my room or even just secretly jog in place when I thought no one was looking. I'm surprised I didn't wear a hole in my carpet. In PE, while other girls tried to avoid sweating as much as possible, I took every timed mile and game of softball very seriously, not wanting to miss any opportunity for more exercise.

I'd come home from school starving and cranky, and hope that my mom didn't notice. I needn't have worried, because for the most part she didn't. She had my brother and sister to deal with, both of whom were still in elementary school, the family was starting to have money problems again, and though she and my dad were back together, they were fighting more than ever, to the point where sometimes I'd have no choice but to round up Mychal and Nickayla and usher them out the door, talking about how fun it would be for the three of us to go to the park for a while.

But by the time I was a sophomore, I started to get the feeling that what had begun as a game had maybe gone too far. One day I was so hungry that I was shaking, and I decided to eat an apple. Instead of eating it, though, I just sat there and held it up to my mouth. I couldn't bring myself to take a bite. It was like the two sides of my brain were competing, one of them telling me to "eat it, it's just an apple," and the other telling me "no, no, no—that'll ruin everything."

My parents were starting to clue in, and I also felt like I was losing control. It turns out that routinely denying your body nutrients and being hungry 24-7 is a great way to bring on a mental freak-out!

I finally worked up the nerve to tell my dad that I thought I was anorexic, which was a slap in the face to my parents. I don't think that either of them had even known anyone with an eating disorder before, and while they knew it was a big deal, they still had no idea what to do about it. At one point my mom even said, "Naya, this is some white-people shit."

When we would all sit down to dinner as a family, I'd go to great pains to hide the food, so that it would still disappear from my plate, even though I hadn't eaten a thing. Our dining table was this big wooden hunk with drawers on the side, which was super convenient for me. When no one was looking, I'd scoop the food into the drawer and quickly shut it again. Usually, I'd come back to get it later and throw it away, but not always. So gross, right? I was like Brittany Murphy's character in *Girl, Interrupted* with the chickens.

One day my mom opened the drawer and found a bunch of rotting mashed potatoes and old chicken breast that I'd stashed in there who knows when and forgotten about. For the obvious reasons, she flipped, and came screaming into my room. She started wailing on me. I was running from her, as she yelled, "What's wrong with you? Why are you doing this? This is sick—this is sick! You need help!" I knew I needed help, and she should probably be the one to help me.

This only added fuel to the fire of our disintegrating relationship. The war between moms and their teenage daughters is an epic one fought in households around the world, and in the case between me and my mom, we both had enough of our own shit going on that we had a hard time putting ourselves in each other's shoes. My mom has never been a great communicator, and she's also a tough-ass lady. It's one of the qualities I admire most in her. But she does struggle with empathy. She's the last person on earth who's going to feel sorry for you, and at this point in my life that was all I wanted. It didn't, and wasn't, going to happen though, and so on the pages of my journal that weren't filled with calorie-counting lists of everything I'd eaten that day and social-climbing plans, I'd scrawl "I hate my mom" over and over.

July 3, 2001

I HATE MY MOM. She's a bitch. I wish she would love me back the way I love her. If she read this, she would probably beat me up. I HATE HER.

July 22, 2001

Journal,

I don't hate my mom. I just don't like her a lot of the time.

At the worst of it, I was five foot four inches tall and weighed ninety-eight pounds. I passed out from dehydration when we had to run a mile in PE—during which I really pushed myself. I had to be taken to the hospital to get an IV. Since it'd already been established that my mom was not well equipped to deal with this, most of it fell on my dad. He picked me up from school and took me to the hospital, and we sat there, mostly in silence, as I got a needle in my arm. "Naya, you've got to eat," he'd say. "I don't know what else to tell you. You're killing yourself." I'd nod, with tears streaming down my face, but then I'd be right back up on my feet after the IV, and the next day I'd throw my lunch in the trash once again.

After an additional hospital visit, my dad seemed to realize that something drastic needed to be done, and that he was going to have to be the one to do it. Someone told him he should take me to see a psychiatrist, so he did, but the visits were as useless as I would have expected them to be.

November 6, 2001

I can't take this. I'm starving! I just had a freakin' breakdown because I couldn't even eat an apple. I don't wanna tell anyone because they'll just think it's old and be annoyed. I don't have a problem — I just suppress my hunger. I can't stop thinking about it — it's driving me crazy! All I think about is what I've eaten today and what I'm gonna eat tomorrow.

Dad would come and pick me up after school, and then drive me to the psychiatrist's totally depressing and incredibly sterile-looking office. I'd sit on the couch and get asked a bunch of predictable questions. He'd ask me over and over again why I'd felt the need to do this, a question that I could readily answer: not eating made me feel in control. I'd already self-diagnosed. I knew why I did this.

If the guy had been worth his co-pay, he probably would have realized that it was my control issues that needed to be addressed here, and that by working on them the eating disorder would probably resolve itself. Instead, he decided that I must be depressed and prescribed Lexapro, an antidepressant. My parents aren't pill-popping people, so I think under normal circumstances they would have balked at putting their teenage daughter on psychotropics, but at this point, they were at their wits' end and willing to try anything that an "expert" told them would work. "I've never dealt with anything like this before," my mom would say. "I wish I knew how to help you."

I was prescribed a very small dosage, but, still, taking the pills made me feel weird, like I was two steps removed from everything around me. I hated feeling out of it, so I secretly started to throw the pills away while pretending to take them. I knew that something was wrong with me, but I also knew I wasn't depressed.

Finally, I told my parents that I wanted to stop taking the pills—which really meant that I was ready to stop having to pretend that I was taking the pills. There was an unspoken understanding among the three of us that since I had gotten myself into this, I would somehow know how to get myself out.

And I did. Toward the end of my sophomore year of high school, I became friends with a group of black girls at school who—unlike the white girls I knew who considered a Slim-Fast bar to be a meal—had no desire to be skin and bones. They preached to me about how guys liked thick girls, with asses and curves. Since at this point in my life, my only guy experience was my twelve-hour relationship with Stewart, I decided that I should probably try to get another boyfriend. These girls were friends with a bunch of jocks, and since there were a couple of guys on the football team I wouldn't mind making out with, that, amazingly enough, was all it took to get me to start eating again. Soon, instead of agonizing over an apple, I was going through the McDonald's drive-thru twice a day. I gained fifteen pounds and never looked back.

THE BIG ONE-EIGHT AND MAKING BIG DECISIONS

My child-acting money had gone into something called a Coogan account, which is kind of like an official trust set up to make sure that your parents don't steal all your money (more on this later). You get access to it when you turn eighteen, and a good portion of my high school years was spent dreaming about what I'd do as soon as I got access to my account—I knew exactly what I was going to do with part of it at least. I'd always been made fun of for being flat-chested, but as long as I was really skinny, barely there boobs were part of the package. As soon as I got "thick," though, I wanted t-i-t-s.

My dad's colleague was married to this diminutive Dominican trophy wife, Erica, who was super cute, fun to be around, and the proud owner of some amazing-looking fake tits. Erica was extra nice to me and took my awkward teenage self under her wing. The first time I ever ate pot brownies was at her house, because she seemed to always be cooking up a batch and let me try one.

She shopped almost exclusively at Barneys and designer boutiques, and the first time I ever went shopping on Rodeo Drive, she was the one who took me. I felt very *Pretty Woman*, except without the prostitution. Her uniform was always sassy little body-con dresses, even though she'd had two kids, and that made her even more of a superwoman in my eyes. I'd babysit her kids whenever she needed me to, and she paid me really well and even let me raid her closet.

She had tons of velour Juicy Couture sweatsuits, which were the absolute apex of LA fashion in 2004, so I'd borrow those and even spritz myself with her perfume, total stalker style. She had already had breast implants, but when she got them done for the second time, I helped out and watched the kids while she was recovering from the surgery. When she came back, she showed me her new toys.

"Wow," I said. "Those are fantastic. When I turn eighteen, I am totally getting my boobs done." Without missing a beat, she handed me a business card and said, "See him!" So I did.

When I became a legal adult, I came complete with a plastic surgeon. As soon as I got access to my Coogan account, I made an appointment for a consultation. I had already told my parents about my plans, but they were—no surprise— staunchly opposed to the idea. I asked my mom to come with me, and in protest she said no. "I do not condone this," she said icily, sitting at the kitchen table with her back to me. I was completely undeterred and just drove myself to the appointment.

At the doctor's, I told them when my birthday was and when I wanted to schedule the appointment, and then I wrote a check for the eight-thousand-dollar procedure so it was paid for before I even walked out the door.

When it came time to have the surgery, I took a week off school. I went around to all my teachers, told them I was going to be out, and gathered up all the assignments that I was going to miss. "Where are you going?" many of them asked, assuming that I was headed on a family vacation to Hawaii or something of the sort.

"I'm getting plastic surgery!" I'd tell them gleefully, then head right back out the door. My art teacher was stoked, though—when I told her, she said that she too had fake tits and that she was very excited for me. "I can't wait to see what they look like when you come back!" she said, which under many other circumstances could be interpreted as totally creepy.

The day of the procedure, my dad decided to drive me. I was living with him at the time, and as much as I don't think he liked the idea, he also knew that letting his teenage daughter drive herself to and from surgery was a guaranteed way to win him the worst-parent award. I was dressed for the occasion, wearing a hot-pink Juicy Couture sweatsuit, UGG boots, and a Tiffany heart-locket necklace. I'm pretty sure this is the official "getting fake tits" outfit as designated by the American Board of Plastic Surgery.

I was not scared one bit about going under or about how painful the recovery process might be. And after the surgery, I didn't hurt much at all, and I didn't even need to take the painkillers they'd given me. Back home at my dad's, I was up and walking around, until he convinced me that I should probably take a pain pill and go to bed, because staying up all night after surgery, as though nothing had happened, was probably not a good idea.

Madison was the first person to visit; she came over to see them and brought me Jamba Juice. My mom eventually came around to my new boobs as well—she had to admit that they looked great, and she started to help me shower and change my bandages, both of which were hard to do on my own.

For a while, I had restrictions on what I could do: I couldn't lift anything heavy or raise my arms above my head, and I had to make sure to massage the implants against a wall so they wouldn't get hard. This looked as awkward and as weird as you might imagine, kind of like a cat rubbing up against a pole.

My new boobs were a confidence thing, not a sexual thing. I'd never even taken my top off for a guy. I hadn't had many opportunities to do so, but even if I had, it probably wouldn't have happened, because my bra was always stuffed with napkins or, if I'd managed to sneak them, my mom's chicken cutlets. Even after I got my implants, it was still a long time before anyone but Madison and my mom saw them. Not that the boys didn't try—as soon as I went back to school, they were all extra nice and practically fell over themselves rushing to see who could hold the door open for me.

When I went to see my art teacher, she was super impressed. "Do you mind if I ask," she said, "who did those?" So I pulled a business card out of my backpack, handed it to her, and said, "See him."

CALLING A TRUCE WITH MY BODY IMAGE

Thankfully, more than a decade after all this stuff happened, I'm happy to say that I no longer treat my body like it's my enemy. Now I love to cook for myself and my family, and since I know how bad fast food is for you (even when it tastes good), you won't find me cruising around town with a Big Mac in my hand. If I went to McDonald's twice in one day now, I'd probably puke.

I have a healthy relationship with food now. I can still lose weight easily, like if I need to quickly drop a pound or two for a photo shoot, or shed my postbaby bulges, but I do it the right way. I might as well make bumper stickers that say "Starvation is not the answer."

I still consider myself something of a control freak, though. It is just how I am—I will never be a go-with-the-flow kind of girl, bouncing around like a pinball. I like to know where I'm going, and that I'm in the driver's seat. I want to have my fall wardrobe sorted out by the beginning of the summer. I know how I want my house to look, and when I have a schedule, I like to stick to it. I think this is also part of why I have such a strong work ethic. I always know my lines, I'm always on my mark, and I'm always on time. I take pride in being professional, and I like to set a goal and work toward it.

As a teenager, though, you have very few outlets where you can decide what you want for yourself. You probably don't have a job, you can't drive yourself, and you're at this weird transition point when the only way you can have any independence is if someone else decides to give it to you. Controlling what I ate was my one way out, the one place where I felt like I got to make the decisions in my life. In my journal, I'd note what I'd eaten that day and what I planned to eat tomorrow. Keeping track and organizing what I ate, and the effort it took to hide what I was doing, felt like a full-time job, which was actually exactly what I wanted. I wasn't acting at all anymore, and I needed to have something that felt like work.

I don't want to trash the idea of going to therapy or taking medication, because that is what works for some people, and both can be very valuable tools. It just wasn't what worked for me at that point in my life. Now I go to therapy semi-annually, because I think it's a much-needed time-out. It helps me to be more introspective, to be more grateful, and to get to know myself in ways that can hopefully make me a better person.

My mom is also now my best friend—I've even read her my horrible journal entries, which now come off as laughable odes to teenage angst and melodrama. I still wish she had been more understanding of what I was going through, and I think she does too, but we both understand why she wasn't. I think you're finally an adult when you can look at your parents as people going through their own shit, rather than just seeing them as unfeeling tyrants here to make your life miserable.

It also seems like body issues are the norm for a lot of women, and I'm sure more than a few people will read these pages and think "that's me!" Being happy with how we look is just something that a lot of us struggle with, and we can name what we hate much more easily than we can name what we love. Some of our parts are too skinny, some are too fat, and some we just hate for no reason. We're always super critical of ourselves, and that also leads us to be more critical of other people as well. You see it in all the tabloids that seem to be chomping at the bit to get a pic of someone bending over in a bikini on the beach, just so they can draw a big red circle around the cellulite. So what? We're supposed to make ourselves feel better by making other people feel worse? It doesn't work that way.

Accepting your body is a lot easier said than done, which is why I think you gotta do what you gotta do to make yourself feel good. People have a lot of opinions about plastic surgery, but more than ten years after I got my boobs, they still make me happy when I look in the mirror. It might have even been the best $8K I've ever spent . . .

SORRY:

- *Wallowing in self-hatred. It's not cute.*

- *Starving myself crazy. This did a number on my physical and mental health, and I owe my body a big apology.*

- *Stashing my dinner in a drawer rather than eating it. (Mom, I am truly sorry you had to discover this decomposing compost heap.)*

- *Shitty communication. Being better at talking things through would have saved both me and my parents a lot of trouble and tears.*

- *Thinking I "hated" my mom. Moms and teenage daughters will never get along—we just have to realize it's nothing personal on either side.*

- *School uniforms. Seriously, they're the worst.*

- *Can duty and falling victim to the school's indentured-servitude recycling program.*

NOT SORRY:

- *Keeping a journal and making lists. I learned early on that writing down your goals is the first step toward achieving them.*

- *Boob job. I thank my Coogan for this cleavage.*

- *Knowing myself well enough to know that I didn't need antidepressants.*

- *Learning to love my body and take care of it, even if I don't think it's perfect.*

- *Figuring out ways to get around can duty (thanks, Dad!).*

NO MONEY, MO' PROBLEMS
Learning to Live With It
and Without It

WHEN I LOOK back at my journal entries, there are several themes that stand out: food (oof), boys (duh), and money. Money was especially important to me as I was growing up, because sometimes we had it—but most of the time because we didn't.

April 8, 2004

Things to do (or buy)

1. ~~get ears pierced (sterling silver)~~
2. pay taxes — $88.00
3. pay Mychal back
4. ~~get clear belly ring while doing no. 1 on list~~
5. get new jeans

6. look for + get guy who fits list*
7. get new eye sleeper mask
8. take back shorts to V. Secret
9. get new bra from PINK collection
10. think about something other than material things
11. get new modeling agency
12. get a job (modeling/acting) — first job in '04
13. do something nice 4 Mom 4 Mom's Day
14. get real diamond belly ring
15. BIG ONE! get Chanel pink C earrings
16. figure out God stuff
17. get new car (nice one)
18. take SATs (get good score)
19. get into good college
20. finally get a record deal
21. get PR person to promote me as hot, sexy, rich party hopper
22. get Tarina Tarantino chandelier kitty earrings
23. take back miniskirt
24. get $71.00 back from Dad
25. finish reading "mind" book
26. get some more money
27. file unemployment claim
28. continue to be spontaneous and everything will work out
29. get some type of shimmer bronze powder for face 4 sexy summer look

*see critera on page 37—38

I once asked my mom why she fell in love with my dad, and her answer was simple: "He was fun." Shortly after they met, she moved out to California to live with him, and I'm sure they were your picture-perfect California couple. She was an aspiring model, and he a surfer boy with long hair and a yellow Jeep. Dad taught Mom how to drive in that yellow Jeep, and wasn't even (that) mad when she later smashed it into a wall.

When Mom found out she was pregnant with me, it definitely wasn't something they had planned on, but they went with it anyway. For most of my childhood, my parents were winging it. We have video of my first birthday party, which was just me, my mom, and my dad (wearing eighties nerd glasses) eating cake and opening presents in our tiny Glendale apartment. Later my dad drove a silver Nissan Z, which at the time looked like it was straight out of *Back to the Future*. It was just a two-seater, so when the three of us were in the car, I'd sit cross-legged in the back, sans seat belt or even seat, hold on to the crossbar for "safety," and duck every time we passed a cop, or even anyone who looked like they might call the cops.

When I was four, my brother came along, and four years after that, my little sister. My parents were no longer two young people madly in love, celebrating their baby's birthday—they had a full-fledged family. Shit had gotten real, and was about to get even realer when my dad lost his job.

We've always jokingly called my dad a jack-of-all-trades. He's a natural-born schmoozer who can fix anything, learn anything, do anything. He worked for Disney, he worked for Universal Music Publishing, he worked in IT, he even drove a truck for a sushi company for a while (my brother and I were not mad at that job, as the California rolls he would bring home were delicious). Some of those jobs paid more than others, and when Dad had money, he spent it. I don't fault him for this—it was my philosophy too. If you're not having any fun now and saving everything for tomorrow, well, hello: you could die tomorrow!

But Dad took it to the extreme: we had boats and two Jet Skis, he had a motorcycle (which I refused to ride because the vibrations from the exhaust made my legs itch), and we vacationed on Lake Mead every year. With three young children, my mom didn't work, so when Dad's money would start to dry up, or a job didn't work out, we'd be back to sharing bedrooms in cramped, shitty apartments and clipping coupons to make ends meet.

When he got offered a job doing IT for a tech company, we thought we'd made it—he was making a really nice salary, and they were flying him back and forth in business class to the company headquarters in Arizona. My parents bought a Lexus to celebrate, and we moved into a big house in Canyon Country. The house was a middle-class dream: two stories, on a lot of land, and located in a brand-new suburban subdivision where all the houses looked the same. It was like something out of a movie. When we went to look at it, I thought it was a mansion.

My brother, sister, and I followed Dad from room to room, asking, "Please, can we have this house? We love this house!" with Mom secretly encouraging us in a whisper, "Tell your dad you want the house."

"WE WANT THE HOUSE!" we screamed in unison from the gigantic backyard. Before we left, Dad put in an offer, and we bought the house.

I had my own room, and I got to have a thirteenth birthday party with a dance floor under a tent in the backyard. The living room had big sliding-glass doors that opened out into the backyard, and my dad opened those and hooked a karaoke machine up to the TV so people could go in and sing whenever they wanted. My mom made chili dogs and ice-cream sundaes, and set up a corner full of beanbag chairs as the ultimate hang zone. I even got to slow dance with my crush. It was movie magical, and the best birthday ever.

Still, though, it was pretty obvious that something wasn't right under the surface. My parents always seemed to be fighting about money, the screaming matches usually brought on by something new my dad had just bought or by the fact that he'd taken out a double mortgage on the house. They spent very little time with each other, and whenever they were both in the house, the tension was as thick as Jell-O.

Then, when I was fourteen, Dad lost the job in Arizona. At first it seemed like no big deal. Dad could do anything, right? Certainly he'd have a new job in no time. As it turned out, that wasn't the case. It was 2001, and I think the technical term for the economy at that time was "in the shitter." September 11 happened, and the first Internet bubble burst, so jobs, especially ones that could support a wife and three kids, were hard to find. We watched as our dad, who seemed like he could talk his way out of a paper bag and who knew enough to be president, couldn't find a job for another three years.

I had overheard enough fighting to know that the double mortgage was a bad idea; but when my parents came home and told us they'd "turned in" the Lexus for a Mazda, it was confirmation that we were indeed fucked.

Soon after that, we said good-bye to the dream house and moved into a shitty three-bedroom apartment that was literally on the wrong side of the tracks. At night, while I was sleeping, I could hear trains rumble by and rattle the pictures on the walls. The other people in the apartment complex were total riffraff, so we couldn't play outside much because my mom was afraid we'd get kidnapped (or worse) by the methy neighbors.

For a while, we applied for government assistance for health insurance, but then putting enough food on the table became a stretch. I also remember going with my mom to the grocery store, where she would write checks that she wasn't sure would go through so she could get some cash to pay for little things we needed and give us a few bucks each to take to school. Christmas was a similar, yet more intense, runaround, as she went to check-cashing places and jumped through all sorts of hoops, trying to figure out how she was going to buy presents for my little brother and sister. Now that I'm a mom myself, I appreciate how hard she struggled to provide for us even more.

My high school was full of rich kids, the kind who got new cars for their sixteenth birthdays and carried Louis

Vuitton Speedy bags to biology class. These weren't kids I was close with, but most of my friends were still middle class. They lived in nice houses and their parents bought nice things for them. Whenever they wanted to do stuff, like go to the mall or watch a friend's band play at a local coffee shop, I had to get really creative to cover up the fact that I didn't have money to go with them. All those acting skills came in handy.

When I was a sophomore, I got asked to go to the senior prom, which seemed like a total coup, until I realized there was no way I could pull it off. I didn't even own any makeup, much less a fancy dress.

When I confided this to my best friend, Madison, she took me to the Clinique counter at the mall and used her own money to buy me eye shadow, foundation, and lipstick. My mom's cousin stepped in to buy me a dress. I was a total prom charity case.

The dress I picked out could best be described as Latina Barbie. It was black satin with spaghetti straps and hot-pink edged ruffles down the front. My mom took me to Santee Alley, LA's wholesale fashion district, and we bought one of those little jewelry packs that had pink teardrop earrings and a matching necklace. I even wore a flower in my hair, señorita style.

In spite of the group effort, the prom was—as almost all proms are—a total disappointment. My date didn't buy me a corsage (his mom ended up running and buying me one at the last minute), and at the dance we barely talked. At the end of the night, he made a halfhearted attempt to sleep with me, which I rebuffed wholeheartedly. The before and after pictures were basically like this:

Before: Me smiling and posing, hair piled high on top of my head.

After: Me scowling and pissed off, with a 'do no amount of hair spray or bobby pins could hold in place.

As Dad's stint of unemployment dragged on, I became the only one in the family who had any money. The California Child Actor's Bill requires that 15 percent of a child actor's earnings be automatically set aside in a trust, which is often called a Coogan account, named after Jackie Coogan, a child actor in the 1920s who earned millions of dollars only to turn eighteen and discover that his parents had spent it all. Whoops.

I didn't have millions—more like tens of thousands—in my Coogan account, but these were dire times. There was literally no money coming in at all, so over the next few years, my mom and I made two court visits to request a withdrawal from my account. I'd miss the first few hours of class, and we'd go to court and stand in front of a judge to petition for permission.

"Your honor," my mom would say, "this is my daughter and she has X amount of money in an account that I protect, but recently our family has fallen on hard times. We would like to withdraw two thousand dollars from the account to cover us for the next month. My husband is currently looking for work, and I have two other children to take care of."

The judge would listen, and then ask me if I was okay with the idea. I always said yes.

Because I'd been a working actor, I was also eligible to receive unemployment, even though I was still a minor. This brought in another seven hundred dollars every two weeks, in checks made out to me that my parents cashed, so for about three years, from the time I was fifteen until I was a senior in high school, I was almost always financially helping my family in some way.

I don't think it's right to take money from your kids, and I don't think my parents thought it was right either. I just think they didn't have any other choice. I wasn't bitter about it at all. Because I'd started working so young, I'd always been mature for my age and had a pretty adult relationship with my parents. But still, we weren't exactly a family that talked things out or excelled at communication, and they never asked how I felt about contributing to the household financially. This was at the height of my eating disorder, and somehow they didn't connect the dots and see my anorexia for what it really was—a control-freak reaction to being under a lot of pressure.

As I've mentioned, my auditions had pretty much dried up by this point in my life, which was a major blow to my self-esteem and sense of self-worth. The added financial stress on my family made me feel even more helpless about everything. Then I felt like it wasn't just my career riding on every audition but potentially the roof over my family's head. And walking in to sing and dance and light up a room while carrying that emotional baggage? Well, hell, it's no wonder I didn't book anything.

When I turned sixteen, I was allowed to take some money

out of the account to buy something for myself—a mother-effing car! Blood, sweat, and tears went into the rounds of negotiation with my parents, and when they finally agreed, you would have thought I'd won the lottery. I set about looking for my dream car, and I found it: a Jeep Wrangler, for sale in Huntington Beach for forty-two hundred dollars. On the day I went to sign the papers, the whole family came along to cheer me on.

The car was a full-on, grown-up version of the Barbie Jeep, no doubt a latent wish hanging around from the days when I got to drive the battery-powered Jeep on *Family Matters*. It was white with two pink stripes down the side, a removable top, leopard-print seat covers, a steering wheel the size of my face, fuzzy leopard-print dice hanging from the rearview mirror, and a pink Barbie sticker on the back.

It was also twenty years old and a bona fide lemon.

The Jeep had no air-conditioning, which I figured was no big deal because I could always just take the top off and cruise around with the wind in my hair. But it was an extraordinarily hot day in June when I went to buy it, and I could already feel the sweat start to pool under my armpits before I'd even pulled out of the lot. I did not care one bit, though—I was on top of the world, riding high on a wave of newly found independence. My family waved to me as I drove off, and as I saw them getting smaller and smaller in the rearview mirror, I was like, "I am free! I am finally free!"

Then my new car started to break down on the freeway. It slowed and sputtered, and all of a sudden there was no acceleration. I put the blinkers on and coasted to the shoulder on the right; then I called my dad to come and get me. Fortunately, I'd only managed to get a few miles, so the family was not too far behind me. Mere minutes after I'd celebrated my independence by leaving them in the dust, there they were, all four in the Mazda, hazard lights blinking and horn honking, pulling up behind me on the shoulder while my little brother and sister waved from the backseat and my mom hung out the window of the passenger side, yelling, "Naya! What happened to your new car?"

There was a feeling of wind in my hair all right—from all the other cars zooming past as Dad and I sweated through our shirts trying to figure out what was wrong. Turns out, the car was out of gas because the gauge was broken. Dad waited with me, while my mom drove to the nearest gas station and returned with just enough gas to get me home. Once we got home, we called the dealership. They were super apologetic and told us they'd be happy to fix the gas gauge. All it would take was another two thousand dollars. That was two thousand dollars we definitely did not have. And there was no way we were going back to court to attempt another withdrawal.

The tears started to well up in my eyes, the smell of exhaust still in my hair from an hour of standing on the side of the freeway. This day was not turning out quite like I'd imagined.

Dad, sensing I was on the verge of a meltdown, jumped up, ran into the kitchen, and returned with a piece of paper and a pencil.

"Okay, Naya," he said, "here's what you're going to do. Every time you go to the gas station, you get a receipt. You figure out how many gallons you put in, and you note your miles from your odometer. Then you divide . . ." I swallowed my tears and nodded. I hated math, but I also really, really wanted to have my own car.

From that day on, I was more on top of my mileage than my schoolwork. I added and subtracted every damn day but still broke down seven times in that car, once when it was 110 degrees in the middle of the summer. I stowed a gas can behind the backseat and made a mental map of the nearest filling stations and the quickest, most discreet routes to get there.

I drove that POS Jeep for two years, and then—wouldn't you know?—jack-of-all-trades George Rivera sold it at an auto fair for thirty-five hundred dollars.

We'd never fixed a thing.

COLD-CALLING MY WAY STRAIGHT TO HELL

I'd imagined that life with a car would mean nonstop cruising to the mall to fill up the backseat with shopping bags, or cute boys piling in so we could all drive down to the beach for bonfires and sunset make-out sessions.

"You guys go on without me," I imagined some dreamy blond surfer saying to his friends. "I'm going to chill with Naya and get a ride [double entendre totally intended!] in that Jeep."

Alas, that was not the case, and my new wheels were mainly used for chauffeuring my siblings around town and picking them up after school, especially once my mom, who'd always stayed home, started to look for work.

Finally, she called me into her room one night when I was seventeen. "I'm divorcing your dad," she said as she sat on the bed. "It's just something I have to do." Rather than crying upon hearing this news, I was happy—for my mom and for my dad, but especially for my brother and sister, who still had to contend with several more years of living at home. This felt like the first step in all of us getting on with our lives. My sister was still in elementary school, so she stayed with my mom, but my brother and I went to live with my dad.

My dad had a few pieces of advice he liked to dole out. One he called boyfriends and girlfriends "dream killers," cautioning us about throwing away our dreams for another person. He was also big on doing what you love for a career (all his children followed this advice), and he took credit scores very, very seriously. "Don't mess up your credit!" was practically his mantra. With every financial decision he made, Dad always meant well and tried to do the right thing for his family. For some reason, stuff just never worked out for him. But he practices what he preaches—even though he's been bankrupt twice, he still has really good credit.

As my eighteenth birthday was approaching, Dad took me to the bank and set me up with a checking account and debit card in anticipation of my getting total access to my Coogan account. As soon as the clock hit midnight on January 12,

2003, my bank account went from zero to forty-two thousand dollars.

Now mind you, $42K is not a fortune, but at that time it was more money than I could even comprehend. My only previous income came from a part-time job at Abercrombie & Fitch, where I made, at most, a hundred dollars every two weeks. The possibilities seemed endless, and Dad tried to steer me in the right direction. He taught me how to balance my checkbook and told me how I could start building up that all-important good credit score by getting a low-limit credit card, using it for a few small purchases, and paying it off every month.

I figured I was set—I really only had a few things I wanted to buy. Forty-two thousand dollars couldn't go that fast. Right?

The first thing I bought was the aforementioned boob job. Eight thousand dollars well spent. Then I wanted a car. I'd talked a lot of shit to the other kids at school—the kind who were gifted Bimmers at their sweet sixteens—about how I was going to get ALL THIS MONEY. "I'm about to come into some wealth," I'd say, and dream about how I was going to crush them with a brand-new (to me) Land Rover Discovery.

I have no idea why I picked a total mom mobile as my dream car, but I could not be swayed, even when the dealership told me my lack of credit history meant I'd have to plunk down a $12K down payment. I didn't care, though. It was worth it to feel the (possibly imagined) looks of envy as I cruised into that school parking lot on the first day. The car should have had a vanity plate that read "COOGAN1."

So with those two "bulk items" checked off my list, I still had quite a bit of spending money left over. I took Dad's advice and got a few credit cards and started to treat myself to a few little visits to kitson.com. And by "a few," I mean daily. Velour Juicy suit? Add to cart. Von Dutch trucker hat like I'd seen Paris Hilton wearing in *Us Weekly*? Go ahead and throw that in there too.

But I was still super on top of my spending, and each month I would do exactly as Dad had taught me and pay everything off. I was also a freak about balancing my checkbook, writing checks for everything and tracking the amounts in the little ledger that came with it. "Minus $15.07 Ralphs," I'd write down, as Madison would roll her eyes and call me an old lady under her breath. But I loved my checkbook (I wish we still used them!), and besides, managing money was fun for me and made me feel like a grown-up.

Those grown-up feelings intensified when Madison and I traded in the T-shirt folding shifts at Abercrombie for a job where we could make some *real* money: telemarketing.

At the time, Madison had this friend Christy (she later turned out to be a total meth head) who was always very speedily and enthusiastically talking about how she was making a ton of money telemarketing and didn't even have to work that hard. That was all we needed to hear to think that this was indeed a great idea.

Soon Madison and I were sitting in a windowless room, manning the phones every day after school. The place we were working was a golf course and RV park that was supposed to be built a few hours away from where we lived. It was touted as an exclusive, all-inclusive retreat where people would come to vacation, play a few holes, and kick back with their families. Our job was to cold-call people and convince them to come to an "information session," where the sales staff would use the hard sell to pressure them to sign up for a time-share membership.

You got fifty dollars for every person you recruited to attend a meeting, and a hundred dollars if the dumbass—er, I mean, poor chap—actually bought a time-share. As clean-cut teenage girls, Madison and I were definitely the outcasts among our ragtag group of coworkers, but we took it just as seriously as everyone else. There was Norma, who chain-smoked and would encourage herself before making calls by growling "I need my money!" There was a black kid who would pretend to be Michael Jordan and sell people on the place's promised exclusivity.

Madison played dumb and acted like a super dippy cheerleader who thought that everything anyone ever said was about the most impressive thing she'd ever heard. "No way!" you could often hear her exclaiming into her headset to some old dude who probably thought she sounded hot. I was super slick and spoke to everyone like we were just two business-minded professionals talking shop. From one hard-working person to another, I knew they would want to take advantage of such a great offer and put some of their hard-earned money to use.

"Dan? Dan, hi, this is Naya from Lake Serenity Golf and Ranch Club. How are you?"

"This isn't a good time. I'm actually having dinner with my family."

"Delicious! Is there a better time I can call you tomorrow?" I wrote down all my calls in my calendar and always followed up exactly when I said I would. "Great! Two p.m. it is!"

And the following day, right on schedule . . . "Hi, Dan, it's Naya from Lake Serenity Golf and Ranch Club. We spoke yesterday when you were having dinner with your lovely family . . ."

Madison and I were so good that we both got promoted. Now we weren't just on the phones but actually doing in-person sales pitches at the infamous information sessions. When one of the owners discovered I was good at public speaking, I got promoted even further—now I delivered the sales presentation. That meant I got a commission for every audience member who'd seen me work my PowerPoint magic and decided to sign up.

I'd stand up onstage in my best business casual attire—little button-up shirts, white jeans, and my kitten heels. With a pointer in hand, I'd click through the slides in my presentation, pointing out where the pool was going to be, the solar panels for green energy, and the view from the eighteenth hole.

"Hey, golfers," I'd say, "I have a question for you—how much is one round of golf where you play?" Then I'd break down the financials of our "birdie package." When I'd exhausted that tactic, I'd go in for the emotional kill, pulling up some stock photos of kids, and saying, "Just think of all the

Kodak moments you and your family will have when you're here." "Kodak moment" was my signature phrase, and I wore it out.

Over the phone, you could really believe that the person you were talking to was a sharp businessman who recognized a good deal when he saw it. In person—oof—it was harder to deceive yourself: these potential customers were usually people with three teeth in their mouth and a credit card, desperately looking to buy into a dream. We were there to sell it to them, and take all their money in the process.

But still, I was eighteen and making fifteen hundred dollars a weekend.

Also, I was totally a believer—I assumed that everything I talked about would happen, that every rendering I showed onstage would someday be built to those exact specifications, possibly even more grand. That pile of dirt there? In my mind, I could already see the bubbling fountain that would someday be in that spot. And there were golf carts! Surely that meant a full course was not too far off.

Wrong. The whole place went bankrupt before a shovel even hit the ground, and Madison and I had to find new jobs. Abercrombie, here I come. Again.

WAIT—SO RENT IS SOMETHING YOU HAVE TO PAY EVERY MONTH?

I paid off the Land Rover, got the good stamp on my credit (just like Dad had said), and swapped it for a little Mercedes

Kompressor. Up until this point, I'd been doing everything right. I still paid off my credit cards every month, and with what was left from my Coogan account and the golf course job, I was the very picture of fiscal responsibility.

When I first turned eighteen, I thought the money would be my ticket to doing whatever I wanted—including ditching my parents and moving out on my own. Instead, I kept living with my dad until I was twenty, and my brother, who was still in high school, was living there as well. Mychal is not a small person.

Also, my dad had decided that since I was technically an adult, and had a job, I should start paying rent.

I didn't exactly agree with him on this point and thought that if I was going to pay rent to live in a bedroom at my dad's house, then I might as well get my own place. I didn't go far.

Valencia is crawling with big apartment complexes, so I literally just looked down the street from where I was living with my dad and said, "There! I'll move there!"

I still love apartments, especially those in big complexes where they all look the same—I find it comforting. I couldn't wait to move in, even though I had no idea how much living on my own would cost. Even though I was now a manager at Abercrombie, I was still making only about three thousand dollars a month—before taxes. I signed the lease and used some of my lump-sum savings to pay the first, last, and security deposit on a one bedroom with a tiny balcony. It was super cute. In fact, thirteen-hundred-dollars-a-month-in-rent cute.

Then I had to furnish it. Aside from my dresser and bed from my dad's house, I didn't own so much as a spoon. I had to buy everything—towels, dishes, trash cans, a toilet brush . . . I also bought a lot of things that couldn't exactly be called necessities—like a Hello Kitty toaster that burned a cat face into each slice of bread, and a giant flat-screen TV to mount on the wall in the living room.

I put all this on my credit cards—fully intending to pay them off—but then discovered that my rent and car payment alone pretty much cashed out my take-home pay each month. Then there were utilities on top of that! I kept paying the electric bill, so at least I could still watch the big-screen TV that I couldn't technically afford, but I wasn't making a dent in the credit card bill, and it was rising by the month. When the bills came in the mail, I didn't throw them away (that would have made me feel too guilty) but stuffed them unopened in a drawer, telling myself that I was going to get to them, someday.

After a few months of living on my own, I was really popular—with the credit agencies. All kinds of credit agencies, all over the country. They'd call, I'd answer, and then save that number in my contacts as "do not answer" so I wouldn't ever mistakenly talk to them again. If anyone had looked in my phone, they would have seen my sheaf of "do not answers" and thought I was up to something seriously sketchy, even though I wasn't. At least not yet.

I lived in that apartment for half a year, and when it was finally just about fully furnished, I had to face the fact that I just couldn't live there anymore. I'd signed a yearlong lease, so I had to pay an early-termination fee, not to mention losing my deposit and paying damages for drilling holes in the living room wall to hang that big-ass TV. When the management company presented me with the final tally of how much it was going to cost me to move out of their building, I practically laughed in their face. It was money I didn't have, so chalk that up to yet another black mark on my credit report.

For my grand move out, I begged Madison to help me, and scraped together enough money to rent a U-Haul. Not an actual truck, mind you, but a flatbed trailer that lets you cruise down the street with all your shit on display in the open air. We hooked it up to the back of her SUV, loaded up all the stuff, and drove right back to the same apartment I'd moved out of just six months before. My dad was coming out the door as we turned the corner down his street. Madison started honking the horn and waving out the window as soon as she saw him.

"Hey, Dad!" I yelled as we pulled into the driveway. "You got room for all this stuff? Don't worry, we'll make it work!"

One reason why I was never too worried about the bills piling up was that I was always hoping an acting job was right around the corner. All it would take was one role, and one check, to pay everything off. This was true in theory, but in reality I was working so much at Abercrombie that I didn't have time for auditions. That impediment soon took care of itself (I got fired), and then I had plenty of time for auditions, but my already small monthly income shrunk down to a big fat zero.

My financial lifelines were unemployment checks and the occasional residual. *The Fresh Prince* and *Family Matters* were both in reruns at the time, so occasionally I'd get a check when one of my episodes would air. It'd be like six dollars, but I'd head straight to the bank to cash it, because, hell, six dollars meant lunch! Some days I wouldn't even leave the house unless one of those checks came. The mailbox and I were best friends. I even requested my own key. "Dad, I've got stuff in there too!" I protested when he seemed ready to resist. "And the bank closes before you get home from work!"

Soon I got more mail—a letter from the bank stating that my car was going to be repossessed. I'd completely stopped making payments on it, so this wasn't exactly a surprise. I asked my dad for advice. "Okay, here's what you're going to do . . . ," he said, and instructed me to clean out all my personal belongings and make sure I always left it where it could easily be found. Clearly this was not his first repossession rodeo, which makes me think that he hadn't really "turned in" the Lexus a few years before.

Now every time I went outside to check the mailbox, I'd also check the curb to see if my car was still parked there, basically like a crackhead making sure no one had stolen my stuff.

Sure enough, one day it was just gone. I texted Madison, like, "Shit, can I get a ride?"

No car, no job was not my financial rock bottom, nor was it the unpaid parking tickets and resulting unpaid court fees that were also piling up. It hit a few weeks later, and completely by accident. I had deposited a twelve-dollar check at the ATM and, without thinking, asked to withdrawal twenty dollars. Lo and behold, it gave it to me and a lightbulb went off: I give machine envelope. Machine gives me money . . .

Soon I was depositing empty envelopes and taking out cash whenever I desperately needed money.

Newsflash: banks catch on to that stuff! And fast.

I tried to play dumb when they called, and claimed I had no idea why so many of my deposit envelopes were coming back empty, but they didn't buy it for a minute. So soon, not only were my credit cards maxed out and my phone constantly buzzing with "do not answer" numbers but I couldn't even deposit my measly residual checks anywhere because the bank had closed my account. Seriously, though, I'm lucky that all I got was a shaming and a few more levels of inconvenience—what I was doing counts as fraud, and I could have gone to jail. There are characters on *Orange Is the New Black* who were locked up for less than what I was doing.

Finally, after a brief stint waitressing—where I seemed to spend more money going out with my coworkers than I made—I realized I had to get serious about my finances.

The first step in that process was facing up to the fact that the big acting paycheck I'd been dreaming about forever might really never come in. I went back to working retail and used the little money I had coming in to pay my dad the rent that he still insisted on charging me. I also started to try to pay down some of my debt—"try" being the key word here, because I was barely making a dent in the interest.

I also cut my expenses wherever I could. I completely stopped spending money on anything that wasn't totally a necessity. I dug through my closets for old clothes that I hadn't worn in forever, and got creative with the styling to make them seem like new outfits. When I absolutely had to buy something new, I bought it on sale, at the store where I worked, so I could maximize my employee discount. When I went to my shifts at the mall, I'd take snacks or pack a lunch, so I wasn't dropping an hour's worth of pay on some shitty pizza and iceberg-lettuce salad from a fast-food restaurant. When the "do not answer" numbers called, I actually answered, and would talk to them about how much I owed where, and what I could do to start paying it off. I always hoped that they'd give me a break because at least I wasn't avoiding them anymore, but, ha! no such luck.

I limited myself to one night out a month with friends, and came to terms with the fact that my new social life mainly involved going over to my mom's apartment to sit on her couch and watch her watch Tyler Perry movies. It wasn't fun, but at least it was responsible. I was no longer afraid that the bank was watching my every move, nor did I feel like a tweaker train wreck, one residual check away from living on the streets.

When I finally booked *Glee*, I didn't celebrate with a vacation, a new bag, or a new ride. Instead, I hired an agency to help clean up my credit. The hard truth about these kinds of agencies is that they really don't do anything you can't do for yourself. The ones you hear advertised on the radio that promise to get negative things "removed" from your credit report are a scam. If you get your car repossessed like I did, well, sorry, girl, that's just not going away.

What they can do is make a whole bunch of calls for you, figure out how much you need to pay to whom and when, and basically act as the intermediary between you and all the people you need to pay off. With my new gig on *Glee*, I had the money to pay off my bills, but the filming schedule was so hectic that I didn't have time to keep track of the bureaucratic side of it, so a credit agency made a lot of sense for me—and I used them for five years.

That was how long it took, and even after I'd paid off all my debt, my credit was still sucky enough that I couldn't get a lease, and had to put down a huge cash deposit when I wanted to get a new car.

Even after I booked *Glee*, I was still cautious about spending money or getting in over my head with any kind of purchase, so I kept living with my dad. Finally, one night I was rehearsing a dance routine for "I Say a Little Prayer" until almost two in the morning, and trying to be as quiet as I could since my dad was asleep upstairs and had to get up early for work, but I kept messing up because I had the music so low that I couldn't hear the beat.

I knew I needed to move out, but there was no way I was making the same mistakes again. I convinced a high school friend to move in with me, and we got an eight-hundred-square-foot studio apartment on Vineland and Ventura. It was a thousand dollars a month, so we split the rent and each paid five hundred. We had two twin beds, like a dorm room, which would have been disastrous if I'd ever tried to bring home guys, but at this point dating was the furthest thing from my mind. I'd work, shower, sleep; work, shower, sleep; and whenever I got a free moment, I'd call the credit agency and see who I needed to write a check to that week.

PEOPLE GET FUNNY ABOUT MONEY

To this day, my mom blames my dad for me squandering all my money, and I'm still trying to reassure her by inviting her over to my house, showing her the pool, and reminding her that I'll be okay. I don't blame either of my parents for the mess I got myself into—my mom came over while I was writing this and was shocked and horrified to learn that I'd put empty deposit envelopes in the ATM machine. She certainly did not raise her daughter to do that.

You have to make your own mistakes, and that's especially true with money. I'd like to think that the fact I blew through forty-two thousand dollars when I was still a teenager was insurance against going all M. C. Hammer with my money when I got older. It's good to get your mistakes out of the way early—as long as you learn from them!

I've always believed in enjoying today rather than squirreling away all your $$$ for the future: if you really want that bag, then buy it, because you never know! But now I take the time to make sure I really want it and that it's not just an impulse buy. If I get sucked into looking at new houses on the Internet, I step back, remind myself that we don't need to move, and try to be content with just rearranging the dining room—cost-effective, and way easier on my marriage.

My mom has always said, "People get funny about money"—and she should know. I was a firsthand witness to the toll financial strain took on my parents' marriage. For this reason, I both hate talking about money and know it's something that has to be done. My husband, Ryan, and I each have our own bank accounts, which we use for personal and fun purchases, and a joint one that we use for bills and everything related to the house. That way if I go shopping, he knows that I'm not using his money to rip and run through Barneys.

After growing up with a stay-at-home mom, I knew I wanted to be an equal financial partner in my relationships. It's a point of pride for me to be making as much, if not more, than my man, but I found myself questioning this resolve when *Glee* ended. I was already into my second trimester, and entering that phase of pregnancy where you can barely keep your eyes open at 5:00 p.m. I couldn't imagine rallying the energy to audition and take on a new role. Also, I'd spent the last six years working my ass off—I wanted to enjoy being pregnant, get everything ready for the baby, and have the luxury of naps. Ryan was totally supportive of this (as he damn well should have been—let's be honest!), and even helped me draw up a postbaby timeline to figure out when I realistically would want to get back to work. In most relationships, the money will ebb and flow, but the important thing is that you're both on the same page about it and have realistic expectations for yourself and your partner.

I've also learned that while you should definitely talk money with your partner, that's about the only person you should be talking about it with. Social media makes it especially easy to flaunt what you've got, but take a step back—do you really want people to know what you've got? No. That's why I'll always keep my bank balance close to my chest, but I will flaunt the hell out of my good credit score. Now, that's something to be proud of.

SORRY:

- *Two words: credit cards.*

- *Two more words: bank fraud. (They can't come after me for this now, can they?)*

- *Spending so much time thinking about what I didn't have and placing so much importance on material things.*

- *Buying cars I couldn't afford. Eff the Mercedes—I should have gotten a Honda.*

- *Wall-mounting a TV in a rental.*

NOT SORRY:

- *That I didn't grow up rich. Having to work for what I want means I appreciate it that much more.*

- *Supporting my family. They mean the world to me, and I'd do it again in a heartbeat.*

- *Getting my financial disasters out of the way early— before I was married or had a family—so the only credit score I wrecked was my own.*

- *Facing the facts and doing little things to save money and cut spending (as opposed to just waiting for a windfall).*

- *Treating myself to luxuries and splurges when I know I can afford it.*

- *About my current credit score. It's really good and, damn, did I work for it.*

FROM BROKE
TO BIG BREAK
The Importance of Keeping It Movin'

HEN I WAS twelve, my mom asked me if I wanted to be famous, and I yelled, "Bring it on!" I was ready—when I was still in kindergarten I'd had a taste of what it felt like to do what I love, and after that there was no going back. But by the time I was a teenager, no matter how hard I tried, fame wasn't bringing me a damn thing.

I hadn't booked a role in years, though not for lack of trying. My pattern was to get to the final round of auditions, make the casting directors love me, get my hopes up, and then have them dashed when it amounted to nothing. I was almost in the Bratz movie—but didn't get it and got super upset. Same with *The Cheetah Girls*.

I also went on more Disney auditions than I can count. A Disney audition meant that you had to sing and dance, so I'd pick my own music, go in there, nail it—and then the part would go to someone else (*cough* Vanessa Hudgens in *High School Musical* *cough*). At one audition, I sang my ass off and had all the casting directors smiling and clapping after I'd finished. "You just do so great every time you're in here!" one of them told me.

I'd heard it all before, and though I'm sure you can't imagine me ever saying anything inappropriate (right?), I blurted out, "Oh yeah—then how come you never cast me for anything?" The whole room went silent, and everyone stared at me as if I'd just told Minnie Mouse to go eff herself. You do *not* talk back at a Disney audition. My mom hustled me out of there as fast as she could.

Once we were outside, I pointed at the big green building we'd just exited, the one that I'd been to so many times before, and told her, "I don't care what they are casting in there—I am never coming back." And so I didn't.

At the beginning of the year, I'd convinced my parents to homeschool me for a while, to open up more time for auditions. But by the time the paperwork went through and we'd gotten the go-ahead to proceed, I was over the idea of homeschooling, and I accepted that the acting thing just wasn't happening. It wasn't as if I could go stand on the street corner and deliver monologues until someone offered me a role on *Ugly Betty*—I literally couldn't do anything unless I had an audition, and those opportunities just weren't coming. I just wanted—gasp—to be normal for a while.

October 20, 2002

I am so upset right now. Because I have to leave school in about a week or so to be homeschooled and I'm really upset. I want to cry. At the beginning of the year, I wanted to be homeschooled because I was having a hard time with my schoolwork, but now I really don't want to go! I won't have any friends, I'll miss out on sooo much! And the worst part is I have to leave because of acting! The one thing that I can't stand! I want to be normal for a while. I'm not even booking right now. It's bullshit!

But my dreams of normalcy didn't last long. I was still determined to keep it moving, so I shifted my focus to music. I'd always loved to sing. We have a home video of me banging the hell out of a Playskool piano and covering Michael Jackson's "Leave Me Alone" when I was only two. I couldn't even say my *L*s—so I was really singing "Neave Me Anone"— but I was pouring my heart out in that song. When I was still in elementary school, my dad would bribe a sound engineer friend of his by giving him a hundred dollars to sneak me into the studio on Saturday afternoons so I could work out my vocal cords on something more productive than just screaming on the playground.

I know what you're thinking: if I wanted to sing in high school, why didn't I just join glee club? Well, I frickin' tried. For one quarter of my freshman year, I was a proud member of the school choir, but all the good solos and parts kept going to my arch-nemesis, Nazanin Mandi. If the name sounds familiar, it's because she's an actress and singer who dates Miguel, but when we were teenagers, she was two grades ahead of me at Valencia High. She got to sing at every damn pep rally! C'mon, girl—give a freshman a break! Because I was totally insane at that time (and, let's be honest, probably really hangry), I decided it was a good idea to challenge her to a sing off. "I don't think she's really that good," I told one of her friends, hoping my dis would travel through the grapevine and get back to her. "You tell her I said that, and we'll sing and see who's better!" It was my most real-life *Glee* moment! Sadly—but probably better for both of us—Nazanin never took me up on it.

Finally, I had enough of playing second soprano and quit. "I don't need to sing 'The Star-Spangled Banner' at a basketball game," I told myself. "I'll just go home and try to get a record deal."

My dad was always super into music, and while my mom had managed my acting career thus far, Dad stepped in to do the same with my music career. He played the guitar, had long hair that made him look like a surfer, loved nineties bands like NIИ and Pearl Jam, and passed on his eclectic taste in music to me.

I had gotten ahold of Robin Thicke's first album and listened to it so much that I practically played it out. But I also loved Modest Mouse, Franz Ferdinand, and, of course, Brandy. Most of my friends were listening to punk, but I just couldn't get into it. While they were dying over Rise Against, I was like, "I'm sorry, but this is the whitest shit ever."

Dad and I soon started making the rounds, pulling on the connections he had from his days at Universal Music and a few people I'd met through acting. Opportunities started to pop up here and there—we went to Atlanta to record, met with Darkchild, a.k.a. Rodney Jerkins, and with producers who'd worked with Omarion and Jhené Aiko. I'd do writing sessions where I'd work on my own lyrics alongside professional songwriters who'd coach me through it.

"Okay, Naya," they'd say. "What do you want to write a song about?"

Um . . . boys? Duh.

And ah, yes, the songs that came out of these sessions—a little part of me is dying of embarrassment just writing about it, and you haven't even heard them. My mom found a demo tape recently, and when my husband tried to play it in the car, my mom sat in the backseat shouting, "Turn that shit up!" while I tried to rip the CD player out with my bare hands.

One of the demo gems is about my best friend betraying me and trying to pick up my man (er, boy?) at the mall. It has spoken-word interludes where I'm saying things like, "Girl, how could you?! We were like blood!" over some smooth-as-buttah R&B playing in the background.

As atrocious as these songs were, they made my dad super proud, and he was convinced we were on the right track. "Writing's where the money is!" he'd say, practically pumping his fist. "You gotta get in there and get a pub deal!"

The entertainment industry has a reputation for being kind of sleazy, but in my experience it has nothing on the music business. Even though I was barely old enough to drive, I already considered myself a professional. Being an actor meant you had to show up on time and know your lines, so I learned to take my responsibilities seriously at a very young age. Yet none of the "adults" we were working with did the same. It was like a whole bunch of drug-dealing car salesmen got together and decided to start this thing called the music business.

"Meeting's confirmed for 3:00 p.m.," they'd say. Then on the day of: "Can you do 9:30 instead? At night." Mind you, I was fourteen, with school the next day.

People who claimed to know what they were doing always tried to coach me on my "image" whenever I had a meeting with someone from a label. "Wear something hip. This is the music business. Image is everything. You have to walk in that room and look like an artist."

Left to pretty much my own devices, I interpreted "looking like an artist" to mean wearing a lot of leather. Specifically, a cropped jacket and bell-bottom jeans with suede ropes that crisscrossed all up and down the sides. I think I wore those jeans to every single meeting.

The meetings themselves usually just involved me and my dad listening to someone brag about all the amazing projects they'd done, or about how someone else they were working with was about to blow up and make a ton of money. Then, when they finally tired of hearing themselves talk, they'd look at me and say, "Okay, sing something."

And I'm sitting there like, "Um, we're in a Jerry's deli . . ."

A few promising meetings did happen here and there. I

landed a small role in a B2K video because we thought it could help me get in good with their manager; but other than earning me a few cool points with the black girls at school, it led nowhere. We also signed a production deal with songwriter Dick Rudolph, and while this seemed like a leap forward at the time, it turned out to be one of many deals that pushed me in directions and genres that sometimes just weren't right and at other times were downright comical. Dick had me do a demo with Al B. Sure!, which had my mom freaking out. "Oh my God, Naya!" she said, fanning herself. "You're doing a song with Al B. Sure!" That's a sign right there that this wasn't going to lead to chart-topping songs—if a singer has the moms swooning, he's probably not the right pairing for a fourteen-year-old girl.

Other deals wanted to push me toward the tween market, but I didn't want my music career to hinge on chewing bubblegum and wearing my hair in pigtails. I wanted to be taken seriously. Couldn't they tell by my bell-bottom jeans?

In the end, nothing seemed right, and by the time I was nearing the end of high school my music career had also ground to a halt. I was officially a regular-ass kid, complete with a lack of direction and affinity for bad decisions.

BEING TOO COOL FOR SCHOOL—AND PAYING THE PRICE

In my junior year of high school, I had somehow convinced my parents to let me stop going to Valencia High and enroll in this alternative school program called Learning Post. My best friend, Madison, had gone into an alternative program that let her earn community college credit. Mine, however, did nothing of the sort.

The program I signed up for was basically a one-trailer schoolhouse that boasted three teachers, a bunch of pregnant girls, and various delinquents and degenerates thrown in for good measure. Once a week, we'd show up for "class" and get some workbook packets that we were supposed to take home and bring back the following week. I'd sold this educational opportunity to my parents as something that would give me more time to go on auditions. However, even though I'd cleared my schedule for them, those auditions did not materialize. Instead, I spent my days sleeping as late as possible, watching daytime talk shows, and generally doing a whole lot of nothing.

Even though I wasn't expending any effort, I was still getting straight As at good old trailer school, so it became obvious, even to me, that Learning Post didn't actually involve much learning. After less than a semester, I transferred back to my old school. Surprise, surprise—that 4.0 GPA I'd earned while doing worksheets didn't amount to much at Valencia High. After I moved over all my credits, I only had a solid C average, but at least I was still eking my way toward graduation—or so I thought. Instead, it turned out that I'd skipped computer applications so often that I'd gone and made myself ineligible to walk with my class. They informed me that if I wanted to leave high school in the dust, I was going to have to take another three months of summer school.

The thought of summer school horrified me and my mom. Mom was pissed at me, of course, for cutting so many classes, but I'd put her through so much during my four years of high school that she was as excited as I was to say "see ya" to the source of so much teenage drama. With me in tow, she marched into the principal's office and gave the staff a sob story that blamed all my absences, not on my simple aversion to computer applications, but on my by now long-resolved eating disorder.

I remember her sitting there in this floral dress and red lipstick and just lying her ass off, telling them that I'd been in the hospital with a feeding tube—which had never happened—and that we hadn't originally informed the school of the severity of what was going on because the family was embarrassed. With her eyes cast down to the floor and her voice lowered to a whisper, she confided in the principal and said, "We need your help to put this all behind us and move on."

That performance right there in the principal's office convinced me that she really had been on her way to becoming a great actress. Except, the principal wasn't buying it. As she insisted there was nothing she could do, my fake tears turned into real ones, and soon I was legitimately sobbing at the thought of having to stay in that hellhole for one second longer than I absolutely had to.

"Come on, Naya," my mom said, as she grabbed her purse and stood up. "I guess some people are just like that."

It seemed like the guilt finally got to the principal, though, and a few days later she called to tell us she'd decided to reconsider, and would let me walk if I could pass a series of tests that proved I had truly learned something after all.

I still consider the day of my high school graduation to be one of the best of my life. For a few short hours, I seemed to forget that I had actually hated most of my classmates. We bounced beach balls from person to person during the ceremony, and at the after party this kid Nick admitted that he'd had a crush on me since elementary school, and we made out. In a car. Clearly, this was an auspicious beginning to post–high school life. One of my relatives even gave me a copy of that Dr. Seuss book *Oh, the Places You'll Go!*

Alas, I did not go far. As you know, the Naya Rivera solo project did not last long when I realized I couldn't afford to live on my own and moved back in with my newly divorced dad.

My brother was still in high school and playing football, so he and I trekked with my dad to the deep Valley—Van Nuys. It wasn't the nicest place to begin with, and our neighborhood was more hood than neighbors. There were no street lights on our block, or any of the blocks around us, for that matter, and it was a bit of a shock to a born-and-bred suburban girl like me.

Dad rented a three-bedroom house for our fractured family and gave me the biggest bedroom. The space was huge, almost like a small loft, and there was plenty of space for all my recently acquired (and unfortunately unreturnable) furniture.

But I had to contend with the five-hundred-dollar-per-month rent my dad began charging me. So I set about looking for a job, without looking very hard. That led me to the Abercrombie & Fitch store in the Valencia Town Center (RIP, because it's long since closed). I had worked at Abercrombie before, as one of my first jobs, when I was sixteen. My friend Madison had worked there too, and it definitely had not felt like "work." It was more like an after-school program: we'd show up for our shifts wearing T-shirts with the name of the store plastered across the front, and sometimes even the back, and cut-off jean shorts so tiny that it was actually a good thing I didn't have an ass. We'd fold T-shirts for a couple of hours, help a customer or two if we absolutely had to, and gossip while spending the few measly dollars that we made on some Panda Express at the food court.

Having a job was so fun!

But now that I was nineteen and had a rent check hanging over my head, I wanted to make more than minimum wage. I figured the best way to do that was to be a manager: I didn't want to fold the T-shirts; I wanted to be the person who told the *other* people to fold the T-shirts.

For some God-only-knows reason, being a manager at Abercrombie required a bachelor's degree, which I definitely did not have. So I just lied—my résumé was a glorious work of creative writing. I explained that because I was an actress, I'd graduated early from high school by taking advanced-placement classes, the kind where you also earned college credit. Because I'd taken so many of those, I had an associate's degree by the time I was sixteen! And just three years later, I'd already obtained a bachelor's degree in—get this—fashion merchandising and communications. I was just that motivated! That someone with a college degree and that much ambition would decide to move back in with their dad and get a job at the mall makes total sense, right?

Anyway, they bought it and hired me, which I guess is probably a testament to my acting skills more than anything. Lies and falsified credentials aside, I was a really good manager—I told all those underling teenagers how to fold those jeans and spritz that cologne like the boss that I was.

One of my coworkers was this guy named Greg, who was actually almost thirty but still acted like he was eighteen. Every season we had to spend an extra late night in the store, changing out all the old merchandise to make room for the new. We'd work until after midnight, and on one such night, I unfortunately hooked up with Greg. In the store (insert grimacing emoji here).

At this time in my life, I'd only had sex once and my amorous adventures were pretty limited. I wasn't used to getting attention from guys at all. It was super boring being in a store counting sweatshirts at 11:00 p.m., and when Greg started coming on to me, I was more "oh well" than "oh wow," but figured why the hell not? At that point, any sexual experience, even a bad one, still counted as experience in my book. Greg and I were one and done, though, and as far as I knew, news of our hookup never really got out.

Then, one day one of my fellow managers called in sick, and someone from a different store came to ours to cover and fill in.

"Who's that?" I asked, when I spotted a girl I didn't know straightening the sweatshirts.

"Oh, that's Greg's wife," my coworker responded. "She works at another Abercrombie store."

I choked on my soda and squeaked, causing my coworker to give me a weird look.

I quickly composed myself for my shift. I had no idea that Greg had a wife—he seemed like such a kid and in no way mature enough for marriage (which he wasn't, obviously). What the hell was I going to do? Now, I had no qualms about lying on my résumé, but I was not a home-wrecker, and my panic about doing the right thing only intensified when I learned that he not only had a wife but also a kid!

To this day, I still get random little checks from Abercrombie, because they're always being sued for some sort of inappropriateness. Even if it wasn't written down on paper anywhere, the stores definitely fostered this idea that their employees were fun, attractive, and sexy, and that working there wasn't work—it was a party! Your shift is practically an orgy! I'm exaggerating a little here, obviously, but I'm trying to give Greg the benefit of the doubt: maybe he didn't wear a wedding ring or regularly mention his wife because he didn't think it was part of the brand. Whatever— what a piece of shit.

I made it through the shift, and later that night decided I was going to call Greg's wife and tell her what had happened. When no one was looking, I did some sleuthing and found her phone number in the employee directory. I didn't want to be a bitch about it, or cause drama, but I knew that things like this get out eventually, and so if she was going to hear it from someone, I wanted her to at least hear it from me. Madison was always my accessory to crime, so we sat in her car, parked in front of my house, as I made the call from her cell phone.

At first Greg's wife didn't believe me, and then our conversation devolved into her calling me a bunch of names and cursing me the hell out. "You are ungrateful!" I finally said, before I hung up.

The next day, though, I sent flowers, sans card, to her at the store. "Why would you do that?" Madison asked. "She just called you a whore!"

"I know," I said. "But I just feel bad! I would never want something like that to happen to me!" Ugh, I still feel horrible just thinking about this whole situation.

I was not looking forward to continuing my working relationship with Greg. But lo and behold, I didn't have to worry about it, because shortly thereafter I was fired for ringing up my own purchase, which in the retail world is akin to outright theft. I hadn't stolen anything, but my new joblessness was a little bit of karma coming my way, and I was more than willing to take it.

For the next three months, I was a bum. I slept late, hung out with my mom, and tried to wrap my head around the fact that I was seriously in debt and had no money. I took one community college class, then dropped it. I was completely lacking direction, and also behind on rent. Soon I owed my dad fifteen hundred dollars, and he showed no sign of letting me forget about it. I decided I would get a waitressing job. The hourly wage wasn't cutting it, and I needed something where I could make tips and have cash on hand every day.

IT'S JUST A RESTAURANT, OR IS IT?

Enter Hooters. In my twenty-year-old brain, I knew I was cute, so I thought: cute + Hooters = better tips. I applied, got the job, and told my parents.

"I don't see anything wrong with that," my mom said. "You're not showing anything. It's just a restaurant." Mom had never actually been to a Hooters.

Dad, on the other hand, had and so was less enthusiastic about my newfound employment.

"Hey, Dad," I said, "you work near the restaurant. Will you come to Hooters for lunch?"

"No," he said. "I will never, ever, come in and watch you work at Hooters."

As it turned out, Hooters may have been a job for bimbos, but it was not a job for slackers. They were incredibly strict about your appearance (I know, I know, big surprise, right?). The T-shirts were tight, white, and said "Hooters" on the front. The slogan on the back summed up the whole experience: "Delightfully tacky yet unrefined." As a waitress, you were not allowed to have stains on your shirt or runs in your hosiery. To add insult to injury, if you snagged your pantyhose in the middle of a shift, you had to hurry back to the break room and *use your own money* to buy a new pair from a vending machine. The signature Hooters shade was "suntan." Let me tell you, it looked great on anyone who wasn't white. (Read: it looked awful.)

Every hour on the hour, they would play a horrible country song on the loudspeakers, and all the waitresses had to stop what they were doing, jump up on the tables, and do a choreographed line dance. Mind you—people were eating at these tables! And that, Mom, is when it wasn't just a restaurant.

My only solace was when Madison would come to visit me, usually because I'd made her. She is pretty much guaranteed entrance into heaven just based upon the number of fried pickles she has eaten in the name of keeping her increasingly depressed best friend company.

One of the other waitresses at Hooters soon hooked me up with a fake ID. It was her cousin's old driver's license, and even though the photo was of a slightly overweight Mexican girl, it either looked enough like me to work, or the clubs where I used it really did not give a shit about underage drinking.

One of my other coworkers was an ex–pageant girl from Texas, and she and her mother had moved out to LA, convinced that this beauty queen was going to be a star. It was from these southern women that I decided to take my beauty tips, and her mom taught me how to do my own hair extensions. We'd buy the weaves from beauty-supply stores, and then instead of sewing them in like normal people do, she taught me how to glue them to my scalp with an incredibly toxic rubber cement that smelled like paint. On top of that, I tried to turn my black hair, both real and fake, blond by dying it myself. It lightened into an awful, acrid shade of orange—you know, that really special hair color that just screams "I buy all my beauty products at Big Lots." I paired this gorgeous styling with a push-up bra, and the overall look may be best described as "budget porn star."

After our shifts at Hooters, we'd hit the clubs in Hollywood—places that had Roman numerals for names or were called just one word, like Noise or Room. The kind of places that preferred their female clientele look like baby hookers. It was through this new crew of girlfriends and our totally classy scene that I met Barry, an older man who was completely infatuated with me. Barry was in his midthirties and would come into Hooters with his friend Steve. Hookers—I mean Hooters—encouraged the waitresses to sit down and chat with the customers. During one such tableside chat, someone invited Barry and Steve to go out with us that night, an invite that they were more than eager to accept.

I found Barry pretty gross, but with encouragement from my friends, who all seemed to have sugar daddies of their own, I let him give me three hundred dollars a month under the auspices of "helping me out." I was still too naive to understand that these financial installments—in cash—meant that eventually Barry was going to expect me to not just look like a prostitute but act like one too.

When it became clear to him that I was never going to sleep with him—probably because I said, "I am never going to sleep with you"—his e-mails and calls became more and more frequent and frantic. I tried lying and telling him I'd found Jesus and turned my life around, but that just seemed to turn him on more. Finally, when I was flat-out scared and felt like I had a stalker, I got up the courage to tell my dad that this time I'd really, really fucked up.

I've rarely seen my dad so mad—at me and at Barry—and he promptly called Barry and threatened to simultaneously kill him and have him thrown in jail. Watching my father do this, and knowing that I'd put him in a position that made him both angry and uncomfortable, was one of the most humiliating experiences of my life.

My whole life was humiliating at this point. There were tons of movie studios nearby, and studio guys would come in all the time and try to flirt with me. No matter that it was the middle of a Wednesday afternoon and they clearly had no better place to be, they'd still try to chat me up in a condescending way. Slurping the wing sauce from their fingers and smiling up at me, they'd say, "Are you an actress?"

Barf. Even when such salacious questions didn't make me throw up in my mouth, I was usually too embarrassed to say yes.

I didn't much feel like an actress anyway. I hadn't booked a part in more than two years, and my auditions had dried up. I wasn't even in college, and the only good thing about my career was that I occasionally got free mozzarella sticks. It's totally normal to be in your late teens and early twenties and still figuring it out and making horrible decisions. But to me, figuring it out just felt like fucking up. I'd been really young when I had a taste of what I wanted to do—everything else was bitter in comparison.

Deep down, I knew I had more in me. If I wasn't living up to my potential, I had no one to blame but myself. I couldn't even blame my dad for making me pay rent.

NAUGHTY IN NEW YORK

By the time I was staring down the barrel of my twenties, life had kicked me in the ass enough to make me think it was time for a plan B (and no, not the contraceptive). My first step toward getting back on track was obvious: get the hell out of Hooters. I quit and threw my stupid suntan pantyhose and that horrible T-shirt in the trash. I unglued all the hair that hadn't actually grown out of my head, and I moved the Wonderbras to the back of the underwear drawer.

I applied for and got a job as a manager at the Michael Kors in the Topanga mall (I lied on my résumé—again—but they were just tiny little white lies). And I enrolled again in community college, this time vowing not to drop any of my classes.

I cut ties with my trashy friends and spent my nights studying. I actually got good grades in all my classes and started to realize that maybe I hadn't given myself enough credit before. I'd fallen back on my looks over and over because I didn't think I had anything else to offer, but now I was starting to see that I was actually smart. Getting a graded paper on which the professor wrote "well written!" felt a million times better than getting a 25 percent tip because some d-bag got to ogle my butt when I dropped off his burger.

In my classes, I discovered that I most enjoyed writing. I started to think about screenwriting as a potential career path, figuring that if I couldn't be in front of the camera, I could at least be behind it. I did some research and came across a three-month program at the New York Film Academy. I gave my dad the hard sell, and he agreed that it sounded like a good idea (he was probably also still thinking that it would be a good idea to get me three thousand miles away from Barry). The program cost ten thousand dollars, and though he didn't have a ton of money, he agreed to split it with me. My mom told me that right before I turned eighteen, she had squirreled away part of my Coogan account to protect it from my spending sprees, and I used that to pay for the other half.

I enrolled in the program and bought myself a ticket to New York—one with three stops along the way, because I didn't want to waste money on a nonstop flight. We had some family friends who lived in New Jersey, and I stayed with them and commuted into the city for class each day. The commute took two and a half hours: I took two buses, a long subway ride, and then walked the final twenty blocks, which, being from California, was probably the most I'd ever walked in my entire life.

Still, I could not have been happier. Even when I was sitting in a smelly seat on a bus going over the George Washington Bridge, I felt amazing. I was finally doing something with my life and making my own decisions as opposed to just going with the flow. I hardly knew anyone, which was also a relief. In LA, it seemed like I couldn't go to Starbucks without running into some guy I went to middle school with or some girl I used to see at auditions.

After a month of that hellacious commute, my friends hooked me up with an apartment in Manhattan, at Fifty-

Eighth and Eighth, which was unoccupied but owned by people they knew, and where I could live rent-free for the next two months. It wasn't really furnished, but I didn't care. When I got my tax refund, I went to Bed Bath & Beyond and bought new sheets for the bed, feeling like a queen. The apartment had no TV, and I could only get Internet in the laundry room. I didn't have much money, but there was a little Mexican restaurant around the corner, and I would go there, sit by myself, and make one margarita last for hours while I people watched.

The first month of the program was all about developing our ideas. We'd come up with several and throw them out to the rest of the group for feedback. I had one idea for a super dark drama that was inspired by listening to Adele's "Hometown Glory" nonstop, but I also had an idea for a teenage comedy that everyone seemed to really like, so I set about putting that one down on paper.

My screenplay was called "Naughty," and it was about two high school girls who are best friends and outcasts. One is slightly overweight, and her skinny friend has stringy hair and wears glasses. Through some twist of the high school rumor mill, everyone thinks they're lesbians, and they decide to go along with it as part of an elaborate plot to get the guys they really like to hang out. One of the girls has a hot older sister who is their mentor and gives them blow job lessons on a banana. The climax (no pun intended) occurs when their parents find out about their doings and stage an intervention, complete with a poster of a pregnant teenage Jamie Lynn Spears with the words "Don't let this be you."

The screenplay was sexy and funny, and I loved watching people laugh out loud as they read it. It didn't feel as amazing as delivering a punch line while the cameras were rolling, but it still felt pretty damn good, and I knew that I was talented. The credits that I earned at the film academy transferred to my community college, so when I got back to LA, I only needed one more year before I could transfer to a four-year school. I'd had such a great experience in New York that I couldn't wait to go back. I started looking into transferring to film school at NYU or the creative-writing program at Columbia. I got a job as a nanny and started to pay down my credit cards and save whatever money I could. I was done with being an actress.

I called my mom to say, "I, Naya Rivera, am quitting acting."

"You can't do that," she said.

"Mom, I can," I said. "I don't know if you've noticed, but this whole thing isn't exactly taking off. I'm drowning in debt. I have to make some money. I need a real job."

Mom still wasn't buying it. "Give it six months," she said. "Go on every audition you can. Don't be picky or think anything is beneath you. Just go, but keep going to school too. Just give it six months, and see what happens."

I felt like I owed it to my mom. She'd put so much of herself into my acting career, and for a while we'd had a really good run. When I was sixteen, I'd told her I didn't want her to be my manager anymore, which was just one example of how I wasn't always the easiest to deal with or the most grateful. My career was as much hers as it was mine. Plus, she's almost six feet tall and a woman to be reckoned with, even over the phone.

"Fine," I told her. "I'll give it six months." This didn't change how I felt inside, though, and I kept looking for apartments in New York the whole time.

STANDING IN FRONT OF YOUR FAMILY WITH NO CLOTHES ON

Mom was right about one thing: I could be picky about auditions, and that was because I secretly hated them. As a kid, I'd been super competitive about auditions and treated the whole thing like a sport. I'd sneak away when my mom wasn't looking and go put my ear up to the door, to see if I could hear those other little girls blowing it. I would listen to my pigtailed nemesis squeak out a song and think, "She sounds awful! I'm the best singer! I've got this one in the bag."

As I got older, though, my confidence became more and more shaky. Auditions are the most nerve-racking thing about being an actor, and the whole process feels like standing in front of your family with no clothes on.

The first part of an audition is a preread, where you just read lines for a casting director who doesn't even pretend to give a shit. Sometimes it's a taped preread, which means you're reading lines for a young assistant with a camera and a lady who doesn't give a shit. Woof. Good luck with your small talk.

If you're lucky enough to make it past that initial read, you move on to a producer session. At this level, the people you read for have a little more invested in the project, so they're cordial and want to joke around and get to know you. You can breathe a sigh of relief, because while you might still feel like you're talking to a chair, at least that chair talks back.

When someone is looking for a certain type, auditions can make you feel like a generic clone. Say you arrive at an audition where they're looking for a girl who is described as "a hot, exotic-looking female." Well, crap—there are going to be twenty hot, exotic-looking girls in that waiting room, so you just have to sit there, trying to not sweat through your shirt and hoping that you're the hottest of the twenty.

An anthropologist or psychologist would have a field day in an audition waiting room, because it is definitely a personality case study. Every comedian exits with the same line: "Well, I just killed it in there, and they told me to tell you that you can all just go on home. Don't worry, I nailed it, so everyone can just go back to their car."

Or all the Chatty Cathys who want to talk the whole time and then, as they walk out the door, feel the compulsion to raise their voices several octaves and screech "Gooooooddddd luuuuccckkkk" to everyone who is still waiting. It's as awkward as it sounds, especially when you've been auditioning your whole life.

Or there's someone there whose birthday party you cried at in second grade, or someone that you know, firsthand, is a horrible kisser.

So for me to tell my mom that I would keep going to auditions even though I didn't really want to, well, it was no small commitment. After she gave me her pep talk, I went on two.

The first was for *CSI: Miami*, a totally cheesy show that I would have turned my nose up at before, if only because deep down I thought I wouldn't get it. The part I auditioned for was a heroin addict who gets electrocuted. My expectations were low, and to prep for the disappointment, I reminded myself that no one would think I could convincingly play a heroin addict. But to my surprise, I got it!

As soon as I was on set, I was myself again. I still loved it as much as I had as a kindergartner. I was completely comfortable and felt at home amidst the wardrobe fittings and the dry sandwiches in craft services and the trip-inducing wires crisscrossing the floor.

In my scene, I'm ambling down the sidewalk in a miniskirt and mules when I'm abducted by a serial killer, who strangles me in the alley before he takes me back to his lair, attaches a few jumper cables to my fingers, and BRRRZZZTTTT. I was on-screen for less than a minute but made the most of it. I screamed and thrashed like a banshee; this was also the first time a part had required me to cry on command. As I walked off set, the script supervisor stopped me.

"You're really good," she said. "You should have your own show."

This was the confidence boost I sorely needed at that moment. Compliments are tricky business: when the people who love you the most and know you the best tell you that you're good at something, it's super easy to dismiss it. "They're just trying to make me feel better," you can tell yourself. "They don't really mean it." But I took this stranger's words to heart: she had nothing invested in me. She didn't have to say anything.

I had gone to the *CSI* audition purely out of love for my mom—my heart wasn't in it. I was finally letting go of the dreams that I'd held on to, white knuckled, for most of my short life.

My mom has always said that what's meant for you is meant for you, and nothing's going to change that. You have to trust the universe, and trust God, that things are going to work out exactly as they should. At age twenty, I already knew that rejection was a huge part of being an actor, but I still took it personally every time I didn't get a part. I'd cry and get depressed, convinced that it was going to be like this for the rest of my life, even when the part I was up for was just a small one. But through all of it, I'd kept going, and that had at least kept me sharp. Even when I didn't care half as much as I used to, I could still put on a good show for the young assistant with a camera and the lady who didn't give a shit.

In addition to *CSI*, I'd only gone on one other audition. I'd cared so little about it that I smoked a cigarette right before I went in, even though I knew I had to sing. As I was walking back to my trailer after shooting the electrocution scene, still high from the script supervisor's kind words, I checked my voice mail. I had one message, from my agent, telling me I'd booked this thing called *Glee*.

SORRY:

- *Hooking up with a married dude.*

- *At-home highlights and DIY hair extensions: some things are best left to the experts, and hair dye is one of them.*

- *Fried pickles. Madison, I am so very sorry.*

- *Thinking my (spectacular) boobs were my best asset, and not my brain.*

- *Accepting "free" money from anyone, ever.*

- *Hooters. Everything Hooters.*

NOT SORRY:

- *Lying on my résumé when I knew I could handle a retail job.*

- *Listening to my mom.*

- *Getting those "figuring it out" years out of the way early.*

- *Being open to a back-up plan.*

- *Getting fired—try everything once!*

- *Three planes, a train, and two buses to get to New York. Hey, whatever it takes . . .*

DON'T STOP BELIEVIN'
The *Glee* Years

W HEN I AUDITIONED for *Glee*, I was annoyed. This wasn't super surprising, because at this point in my career, I hated auditions (still do, actually), but this one also involved driving out to a music store in Van Nuys to buy sheet music. Annoying errand aside, it did seem like one of the cooler auditions I'd been to in a long time because it involved singing. If I booked the role, it would be really awesome to be able to combine the two things I loved the most, but that was a big "if." I'd gotten really familiar with "if" over the last few years and wasn't counting on anything anymore. In fact, I so wasn't counting on it that I stood outside, smoking a cigarette, right until it was time for me to go in and belt out Destiny's Child's "Emotion" (my choice) with all the runs included.

The character I was auditioning for—who would turn out to be the unforgettable Miss Santana Lopez—didn't have any lines in the pilot, so I auditioned by reading Mercedes's lines. It was a whole bit about how hard it was to get stank ass out of polyester, and I made sure to add extra panache.

Even after I booked it, I still wasn't that excited—it was just a small role, and in a pilot episode. There was no telling if the show would be picked up or if I would be asked back if it was. When I showed up for the first day of filming, I walked into the production office and noticed that there were *Nip/Tuck* posters hanging everywhere. I was a huge fan of the show, and during one of my stints of unemployment, my mom and I had watched every episode together.

"Why are there *Nip/Tuck* posters everywhere?" I asked the kinda cute guy (who I would later make out with) behind the desk.

"This is Ryan Murphy's office," he said snidely.

"Who's Ryan Murphy?" I was clearly winning him over.

"The creator of *Nip/Tuck*. This is *his* show." I sucked in my breath, and ran outside to call my mom. Now, in spite of my best efforts to remain cool and not get too attached to the show, I had to admit that I was more than just kind of excited.

It's crazy now to look back and think about how much time we had to rehearse in the early days, when a lot of the cast was just getting used to doing choreographed numbers. We'd work on one song for an entire week, whereas by the final season of the show, we'd run through it just a few times and then be ready to roll. Since Santana wasn't part of the

112

glee club in the beginning, she wasn't in the iconic opening number—a rendition of Journey's "Don't Stop Believin'" that blows their teacher, Mr. Schuester, away. The actors who were a part of that number had already been rehearsing together for a while.

I remember watching them as an outsider (much like my character would later in the show), and being kind of jealous of the bond they'd clearly already formed—they had all these inside jokes, like about how Cory couldn't dance. My feeling like an outsider changed quickly, though, when I met Dianna Agron, who played my fellow cheerleader, Quinn, and who also hadn't met anyone else yet. Dianna and I had all our scenes together, and we were instant friends. The trailers on set during the pilot were super small and divided in two. Dianna and I shared one, and we soon decided to take down the partition that separated it so we could make a bigger shared space.

I tried to think of ways I could make Santana stand out, even though she didn't have any lines. I figured that if she was the bitchy sidekick, then I was going to make her a megabitch with extra kick. There was a big scene in the choir room, with a bunch of students sitting in chairs, and I was rolling my eyes and popping my neck at every joke. And I guess it must have worked! Ryan Murphy shot the pilot, and between scenes one day, Dianna and I were walking in our Cheerios uniforms when Ryan came up to us and said, "You should learn 'I Say a Little Prayer.'"

"Okay!" I said. "What's that?"

"A song. You might be singing it in the next episode."

Then he walked off.

Dianna and I turned to each other, eyes open wide, but tried to play it cool. Next episode? That meant I was coming back! And not only did I have lines, but also an actual song!

At first the show used two real high schools, one in Long Beach and one in Burbank, as stand-ins for McKinley High, so showing up to shoot felt like actually going back to school, with the football fields and linoleum-tiled hallways lined with rows of lockers. When wardrobe first handed me the cheerleading uniform, I was stoked. One, because I'd never played a cheerleader before, and two, because I was relieved that I got to wear a costume that made me look hot. I remember trying it on and doing a little jump when I looked in the mirror. I had no idea that I'd be wearing that same damn uniform for pretty much three years straight! My first scenes were all classic mean-girl shit, making fun of Rachel. My first line was a snide, tossed-off "get a room" as I walked by Will and Emma talking in the hallway.

Then the rest is bitchy history.

From the very beginning, we all knew that there was something special about *Glee*. For one, there weren't any huge names attached to it. It wasn't a show that just banked on an established star's personality, and that meant people who watched it got to know the characters first and the actors second. I think that's why *Glee* resonated with so many people. The show's acceptance of all types of characters who lived all types of lifestyles made kids in real life feel more accepted. For a lot of people, I think *Glee* was the first show that made it possible for them to turn on the TV and see someone who looked like them or who was dealing with the same kinds of issues they were dealing with. Plus, we weren't just a bunch of actors playing a band of misfits on TV—we really were a band of misfits. And we were inseparable.

LIVIN' LA VIDA LOPEZ

We were all super young when we started—like twenty-one or twenty-two, and baby Chris Colfer was only nineteen— and for all practical purposes, we were still kids. Going to work was like going to school, except we got paid to be there, and there were real consequences if we skipped. Oh, and I had people to talk to, rather than spending every free moment on the phone with my mom so I looked popular.

Our call times were often brutally early in the morning, and everyone quickly fell into the routine. Some people would be in a horrible mood because it was so early, and others would be disturbingly cheerful. As soon as we hit hair and makeup, we'd start talking to one another, and no one would shut up for the rest of the day. Actors tend to be extroverts, and at least twenty times a day someone would do

Some of the greatest people I've ever called friends.

something that would have me laughing so hard that I'd be red in the face and unable to catch my breath.

Kevin McHale would always make weird faces. He did this one character he called Phil, where he'd contort his face until he looked weird and creepy. In the middle of scenes, Kevin would have his back to you, but then he'd turn around and there was Phil. Every time he did it, I thought Jenna Ushkowitz would pee her pants she laughed so hard. I also have video of Mark Salling skipping across the choir room, clapping his hands, and chanting, "Eat your veggies, kids! What makes you different makes you special!" because he thought our show had the morals of an after-school special.

Glee was quick and colorful, and shot in a way that was snappy and in-your-face. Everyone loves teen drama, and *Glee* pulled it off with a twist. All the characters had surprising sides to them, and the dialogue was laced with witty one-liners and double entendres. In what other show would I get to play an underage cheerleader who tells John Stamos, playing a dentist, "You can drill me any time"?

When the show first started, we'd have an entire week to rehearse dance numbers and get the choreography down. We'd rehearse at this dance studio on the Paramount lot called the Tin Shed, and a shed was just what it was—the AC once broke and we still had to spend two days dancing in that sweat box, rehearsing for an episode with Kristin Chenoweth. Lea Michele kept threatening to call SAG about the unsafe working conditions. For once, Lea and I were in total agreement. Zach, our choreographer, has video of me where I turn around and stare straight into the camera with sweat dripping down my face. "I hate this dannnnccccceeeee . . . ," I growl.

"It's not even a dance, Naya," he says. "It's just eight counts!"

Heather Morris and Harry Shum were the best dancers by far, since they were professionals, but it was hard to pick who was the worst—because there were so many of us who were just really, really bad. Cory would get super frustrated, and I remember one year when we were rehearsing "Paradise by the Dashboard Light" for a sectionals performance, he huffed and puffed his way through it and kept threatening to throw up. Luckily for him, he was often the lead, so eventually they'd just let him stand there and sing while everyone else danced around him.

Kevin was a pretty amazing dancer, even in a wheelchair— go figure. Chris Colfer was good at picking up choreography but didn't have the best rhythm, so he eventually convinced the choreographers to let him use props, like brandishing a sword or swinging from the rafters in a cat suit.

Singing and performing in *Glee* was exhilarating and exhausting, especially for me, because I still get stage fright. Being on stage was usually fine, but performing in the choir room was actually far more nerve-racking. It's 6:00 a.m., you've only been awake for an hour, and you're the first person up. Some people are still scarfing down eggs, or sleeping while sitting up, and you're there to belt out a really emotional song. And I knew that they were all secretly judging because—duh—that was exactly what I did too.

The first major song I got to perform was a duet of "The Boy Is Mine" with Amber Riley, and the whole thing stemmed from a joke. Ryan Murphy was a big fan of my Monica impression—I'd sing the song with all the warbling sass that she had, and Ryan was always randomly walking on set and requesting that I do it.

I made him laugh enough that he finally wrote it into the script. "Do you want me to sing it like me or sing it like Monica?" I asked, and we settled on half and half. It's still one of my favorite numbers. Long live nineties R&B.

On-screen, Santana bedded Brittany, Finn, Puck, and Quinn (though the cameras only showed them cuddling postcoitally). In the Madonna episode, Santana took Finn's virginity to "Like a Virgin," and seduction to a song was about as awkward as one might imagine. Cory and I didn't know each other that well at that point, but I had to crawl up his leg and pull his shirt and throw him on the bed and start grinding. He was supposed to chase me around the bed and pick me up and spin me, but I think he was a little hot-and-bothered/nervous about the whole thing, because everything was a little off. Instead of a slow spin, he picked me up awkwardly and turned around so fast that I practically got whiplash. "Oh, okay . . . ," Zach would say. "Let's try that again . . ."

But by far the worst scene I ever filmed was when Santana had to kiss the kid who had mono. One: we were shooting first thing in the morning. Two: they kept spritzing him with glycerin so he'd look extra icky and sweaty. Three: actual, real DNA-containing spit kept transferring from his lip to mine on every single take, and I swear he was doing it on purpose.

In the beginning, Santana and Brittany, Heather's character, were just allowed quick pecks, because the writers had to assure the network that they were just dipping their toes in the gay pool. But as their relationship progressed, hookup scenes with Heather could also be pretty uncomfortable (though she never spit on me), especially when we were supposed to be in Love with a capital *L*, making out and then dropping jokes like, "Oh ha-ha, isn't scissoring just great?" And at this point, Heather was a mom . . .

The biggest kiss we ever had was in a scene right before Santana and Brittany's wedding, where the stage direction in the script said something like, "They share a kiss they can't have in front of everyone else." Brad Buecker, who was directing the episode, came up to us beforehand and gave us this bit of direction: "You know," he said, "just really go at it." I guess I did it right, because my mom screamed when she watched the episode and thought I really had stuck my tongue down Heather's throat. (FYI: I didn't. The trick is you go in with an open mouth, then close it as soon as you make contact.)

Like many things that went on to become major plot lines on *Glee*, Brittany and Santana's relationship started out as a joke. Late one season, Brittany made reference to the fact that she and Santana had hooked up. It was a casual line, and later I asked Brad Falchuk, who'd written the episode, if Brittany and Santana really had a thing. "Well, I don't know," he said. But when we came back from hiatus, he'd figured it out: Santana was a lesbian.

At first, I was just happy that she was getting a story line (because, hello, more screen time for me), but as that story progressed, we all started to see how much it was resonating with people. It was no longer a joke or a way to spice things up but something that we should take seriously. As each new episode aired, I would get tweets from people thanking me and telling me how important the story line was to them. The writers would get similar praise—and also the occasional death threat from a lesbian warning them that they'd better not mess this up. I think we did a pretty good job; Santana and Brittany were able to show that a gay relationship was just that—a relationship, with no less or more of the ups and downs that happen in any relationship.

With Santana, I hit my stride after season two. In the beginning, she was super young, so her mean streak and cattiness were very typically high school—her insults were pointed and she looked for obvious weaknesses, like when she tells Rachel, "Nobody ever tells you anything because (a) you're a blabbermouth, and (b) we all just pretend to like you." Ouch.

I think people connected with her because everyone loves a good "tell it like it is" person, the only one who says what everyone is thinking. The more Santana's character developed, the more she started to toss off insults casually, saying them as if she didn't care if they hit their mark. This effect often made them funnier—and even more insulting.

Being from Lima Heights Adjacent, she was hot-tempered and emotional, but as she grew up, I learned how to show that she internalized pain—no sobbing necessary. I felt like

I was growing up with the character because offscreen my life was changing just as much as hers was on-screen. As the show progressed, you could see her come to terms with her own issues, and the more she understood herself, the nicer she was to be around. In the beginning, Santana was a man-eating cheerleader with a chip on her shoulder; in the end she was married to her best friend and truly cared about people. Similarly, I ended *Glee* happily married with a baby on the way.

OFFSCREEN BONDING

When the cameras weren't rolling, the cast and crew were just as close-knit and the dynamics just as messy as they were on-screen. Between takes or during set turnarounds, we'd gossip and rehash our weekends or pick apart a date that someone had been on. We were all super involved in one another's lives—sometimes maybe a little too much. After a brutal week of nonstop rehearsing and shooting and twenty-hour days, instead of all going our separate ways and heading home, we'd hang out in someone's trailer and play spin the bottle or truth or dare, or we'd just go out to dinner.

In the second season, Kevin and Jenna became room-mates, renting a house together, which became our ground zero for hanging out. We nicknamed it the Love Nest, after a tabloid rumor claimed that Kevin and Jenna were dating and had "shacked up in a Laurel Canyon love nest."

But what happens at the Love Nest stays at the Love Nest. Though, trust me, I know everything that happened at the Love Nest because I was the unofficial third roommate, there every day, no invite needed. Kevin and Jenna didn't mind, because it meant there was always an audience for Kevin's impromptu, full-on dance performances around the living room.

The Love Nest was also where we got one of our castmates high for the first time, or at least tried to. We fed him a whole bag of weed gummy bears one New Year's Eve, and he still didn't feel a thing. We even got Lea up to the Love Nest, and Lea does not go out. She wanted to let her hair down, so she drank two hot toddies while she was there. The rest of us were slamming champagne and vodka, and Lea's in the kitchen making tea.

In these early seasons, we definitely spent as much time hanging out together as we did working—and all we did was work. We would all go sing karaoke, we never missed a birthday (or other reason to celebrate), and we got dressed up and did something stupid every chance we got.

Kevin and our friend Telly Kousakis, who had started out as a production assistant on the show but quickly morphed into everyone's new BFF, nicknamed me Snix, because they said Snix was the name of my alter ego, who only decided to show up when I was drunk. Snix was apparently off-the-charts sassy, whereas regular old sober Naya just registered about an eight or nine. Snix became such a hilarious topic of conversation that one of our producers even worked her into the show as Santana's alter ego.

Every year, I'd throw a Christmas party called Snixmas. I freakin' love the holidays, especially decorating my house for them, so I'd go all out for Snixmas. When I lived in Beverly Hills, I rented a giant machine that blew fake snow all over the front of the house, so it was goose-bump-inducing chilly as you walked up to the door. The inside was full of cinnamon candles, warm whiskey, and Christmas carols sung by real carolers. I had little people dressed as elves passing out champagne, and covered the pool so it turned into a dance floor that was made to look like an ice-skating rink. The neighbors loved it. Or, wait, I'm sure the neighbors would have loved it, if they'd been invited. Again, whoops.

One of our makeup artists also threw a giant Halloween party every year. We'd get as many people as we could together for a group costume, and then rent a party bus so we could stay together all night. We may have been partiers, but we were responsible partiers. Also, we could just imagine the TMZ headline: "Entire Cast of *Glee* Dies in Drunk-Driving Accident While Dressed as *Looney Tunes* Characters." Yeah, no . . .

One of my favorite group costumes was when we were the *Rugrats* characters. None of us broke character all night—we even drank all our booze out of baby bottles and sippy cups (it's surprisingly convenient—no spills!). Kevin was baby Dil, and we pushed him everywhere in a stroller. Dianna was Reptar (major props to Dianna for bucking the "girls just wanna be sluts" Halloween stereotype and wearing a head-to-toe fuzzy dino costume that was not sexy in the least). Harry and his girlfriend were Phil and Lil, and Telly—who is a not-small man, with facial hair—was Angelica. Telly made a beautiful toddler. One of our writers was the dog, Spike, and I, of course, was Susie Carmichael, one of the few ethnic *Rugrats* characters.

We had an iPhone boombox cued up to the theme song, which we blasted to announce our arrival, and carried a playpen. Everywhere we went, we'd set it up in the middle of the room (other partygoers be damned) and climb right in. In pictures, I am so drunk that I'm cross-eyed, sitting there in that damn playpen. After the party, on the way back to the bus, Kevin toppled out of his stroller and was as helpless as a real baby. It took about five of us, over the course of at least ten minutes, to get him back in. Yes, he could have just walked on his own two feet, but where is the fun in that? I think this might have been the moment when I realized how much I loved Kevin McHale and that we would be friends for the rest of our lives.

I also hung out a lot with Dianna outside of the group. Dianna was born fancy. She's like Madonna—one day, she'd show up with a British accent, and you wouldn't even question it. Because, hello—it's Dianna. I nicknamed her Elizabeth Taylor because of her many male suitors (which I entirely approved of—have you seen how hot some of the guys she's dated are?). We traveled by ourselves, and the first time I ever went to Paris was with Dianna. We were in Europe for the *Glee* tour and had two days off, so were like, "Screw it, let's go!"

Dianna wore a pink wig the whole time, and talked to everyone and got us into all these swanky places—not because anyone knew who we were, but just because she worked her magic on them and charmed us right past the velvet ropes. We wandered the side streets, shopped at markets, and hung out in cafés with art students. We smoked nonstop (when in Paris . . .), ate ham-and-cheese baguettes, and drank white wine out of a box. *Oui, oui, oui*—it was truly the perfect way to do Paris.

The *Glee* tour was an intense experience for all of us—it was alternately exhilarating and exhausting. This was probably a good thing, because I was just too tired most of the time to realize how monumental it was or how big the venues were. I can get stricken with stage fright—that kind of "I'm going to puke" feeling that's accompanied by sweaty pits. But when we performed in the Staples Center in Los Angeles, which is the arena where the Lakers play, I somehow thought it was no big deal. A few years later, I went there to watch a show and was in awe of how big it was and how many people were in the audience. Had that registered when we performed there, I probably would have passed out from fear.

There were times when we knew how special *Glee* was, but for the most part, day in and day out, it was a job. It took a lot of mental focus and a lot of physically hard work. I didn't have time to think about the bigger picture, but the tour was when it hit me. The show was a full-on phenomenon and I had fans. Holy shit. At a show in Manchester, our choreographer came backstage and said, "Naya, you should go outside—there's a girl waiting and she has a tattoo of your name." I did not believe him until I went outside and there she was. I was pretty flabbergasted, like, "Are you sure you wanna . . . Maybe you shouldn't . . . Oh, wait, you already did . . ." But I gave her my comp tickets for the night so she could at least get free, really good seats for the show.

We made the most out of our downtime as we traveled through all sorts of random places, and after the shows, we'd hang out in one another's hotel rooms, staying up all night and goofing around. There was not a lot of sleep happening. One of the ways we would pass the time was by putting on what we called "Mousterpiece Theatre," which was our version of a weird talent show. On Kevin's birthday, we all gathered in his room to celebrate—he was the "mouster of ceremonies" and wore a cape made out of a bedsheet. He would call upon people to entertain him, and whomever he picked would have to jump up and perform. Heather did a dance in her panties, and I'm pretty sure Cory had a hard-on the entire time. No dis on Heather, because I also did a dance in my panties.

We were just that kind of cast.

REMEMBERING CORY

The night of Kevin's birthday "Mousterpiece," Cory and I took a break and sat on the balcony smoking a cigarette, just the two of us. The conversation turned to why we'd never made out, maybe because he was fresh off of seeing me gyrate in my panties.

"How come, out of everybody here, you and I never hooked up?" Cory asked, passing me the American Spirit we were sharing.

"I don't know, Cory," I said. "I just don't see you that way."

"We've never even kissed!" he protested.

I leaned over and pecked him. "There you go!" We laughed, and never brought it up again.

Minus that one incident of kissing, Cory and I had a very brotherly/sisterly relationship, which was rare in a cast that had the sex drive of bunnies and the bed-hopping skills of a polygamist cult. There was no pretense, and I think that made us closer. We were just bros—which was especially funny considering how often our characters insulted each other on-screen.

One summer I spent a ton of time at his house. If I was bored, my car would just automatically point itself in that direction—I didn't need to call ahead but could just drop by and Cory would be welcoming and happy to see me. He had a million friends, and there was always a BBQ going.

That summer he'd rented a giant mansion in the Valley that looked like it was straight out of *Scarface*. It was pure marble and glass. He was always having pool parties, which was entirely unsafe, because every surface in the place was slippery when wet. It was amazing that heads didn't crack open on a daily basis. I'd tiptoe across the puddled tile, always convinced I was one misstep away from death.

In the beginning, Cory was really open with all of us about his past and the problems he'd had with drugs and alcohol. He flat-out said, "I am a former addict," and he didn't drink or do any drugs. As far as I know, he was totally sober up through season three. After work one day that season, he and I went to this rooftop restaurant at the Hotel Wilshire. We sat there for four hours, talking and laughing. I'd just finished a scene where I had to cry, and he complimented me on how real it was. He asked, "How do you just start crying?"

"I dwell," I said. "I'm a dweller. Use your shitty experiences. It's like therapy, and it's awesome."

"Oh man," he said. "I can't do that. I can't go there. You want to know what I do? I open my mouth for a really long time like I'm gonna yawn, and it makes my eyes water." It was a sweet moment, but I look back and wonder what kind of pain he was blocking out, even then.

When we were shooting the last episode before going on tour, a bunch of us went out to dinner and decided to celebrate with cocktails because we knew we were going to be working until the wee hours, and there'd be no time to do it later. It was also Cory's birthday, and when he decided to order a cocktail, it was the first time we had ever seen him drink.

He noticed that we noticed. He explained that he wanted to be able to drink in moderation, that he could do it and be just like everybody else. He seemed calm and confident about it, so we all just accepted it. To be honest, I don't think many of us really understood how addiction worked, nor did we fully realize the extent of his former addiction.

I always thought of Cory as a recovering alcoholic, and completely forgot that he had also had a heroin problem. I guess he hid it well. I thought of heroin as a problem that was relegated to strung-out junkies who lived on the street, not my sweet, smart, talented friend who had plenty of money. He always knew his lines and choreography and was wide awake. Heroin was the opposite of awake.

When Cory and Lea started dating, it was a total surprise. The more serious they got, the less Cory hung out with us, and the more he seemed like a different person. One year he came back from the break between seasons super skinny. He said he'd been spending a lot of time at the gym and was trying to be responsible—not spending money all the time and buying crazy cars like he used to. My personal feelings for Lea aside, I knew that she wasn't a partier, so I felt like maybe their relationship could actually be good for him. I was happy for Cory to have a stable influence in his life, wherever it was he found it.

A few months later, I was in London because my then-boyfriend Sean was performing at the Wireless Festival. It was after midnight and we were asleep in the hotel when my phone started ringing. Finally, I picked it up, and it was Telly, sobbing uncontrollably.

"Naya, Cory died." I was shocked, and made him repeat it several times before it sunk in. Telly was inconsolable but also, as anyone who's ever lost someone to drugs can identify with, angry.

"He died of a heroin overdose. Those fucking drugs! I knew it! I knew it, those fucking drugs!"

This also became a defining moment in my relationship with Sean—I started to realize that I was dating an incredibly selfish person. I shook Sean awake and told him that Cory had just died. He just said, "Oh man, babe, I'm really sorry about that," and rolled over and went back to sleep. I was crying, and kept coming in and out of the room as I went out into the hallway to make phone calls, and he never got out of bed or even so much as sat up and turned on the light. This still blows my mind to this day.

Kevin just happened to be in London as well, and the news reached him at the same time. I got him on the phone and just sat in my pajamas on the hotel's hallway floor, with him doing the same across town. We didn't say much, and mainly just listened to each other cry. Finally, we had to decide what to do. Sean's show was just a few hours later that day, and we decided we'd still go, mainly because we didn't know what else to do. Kevin came and met me, and at the show we stayed backstage the whole time so no one would see us.

I had booked a week in London before I was scheduled to do an appearance in Italy, and Sean was going to be there the entire time as well—it was supposed to be our vacation. The next day, though, he decided to fly out early due to an undefined "schedule change," leaving me alone in London. There were paparazzi camped outside the hotel, and I couldn't do anything. I don't mind being alone in cities, and normally I would have just shopped and gone to see the sights, but I didn't want to be photographed "living it up" when my friend had just died, so I camped out in my hotel room, like Eloise, drinking tea and eating biscuits and crying.

Everyone deals with death in their own way, and some are better at it than others. In showbiz they always say "the show must go on," and that's true, but with *Glee*, we barely got a moment to breathe at all. Filming "The Quarterback" episode was one of the hardest, most emotional things I've ever done. I understand that the episode was created from a place that meant well—it was supposed to be our way of paying tribute to and mourning Cory on-screen, but most of us hadn't gotten a chance to go through that process yet offscreen. Everything just happened so fast—after one take several of us were bawling and trying to pull ourselves together when someone popped their head in the room and said, "At least you guys are acting, right? It's not like it's real life. Great job!"

The one thing that did make me feel good about this episode was that Santana had a big part in it. I think that was the writers' way of acknowledging the friendship Cory and I had, and since Lea was in no place emotionally to take the lead, they thought I was the next choice to step in. Mike O'Malley wrote me a very sweet note, telling me how he felt that people looked up to me on set, and that I needed to be extra strong to help pull everyone else through it. That was really comforting, and I tried, Mike, I tried.

From the outside, Cory's life looked perfect—money, fame, beautiful girlfriend, millions of adoring fans—but I guess his same old demons were still there, raising as much mental and emotional hell as they always had. Maybe even more, now that everything was supposed to be okay. I think this is a common misconception about fame, or any kind of marker of "success" in life, be it landing your dream job, getting married, or having a kid: people think that you achieve these goals, you check off certain boxes, and all of a sudden life's perfect and you don't have any problems. That's not true. You're still going to wake up every morning, and your problems will still be there unless you figure out a way to make them go away. And more often than not, new ones will show up in their place.

I still think that Cory had so much to live for, and for me that's the worst part about his death—that it was so unnecessary. I miss everything about him. I just miss his life, and I wish that he was here, experiencing in his own life the kind of things that I'm experiencing now in mine. A calm after the storm, if you will. Everything about his death seems unnecessary.

I doubt I'm alone in feeling a lot of regret about his death. Since he died, a lot of us have spent time wondering and talking about what would have happened if someone had stepped in or confronted him about what was going on.

Or what if he'd been trying to talk to someone about what was going on and just thought no one cared? Like, maybe that one time when it was just the two of us walking out to our cars, maybe if I would have just walked a little bit slower and hadn't been in such a hurry to get home, maybe he would have seen it as an opportunity to bring something up. You can drive yourself crazy thinking like that, because no number of ifs will ever make anything different. Yes, we were a close-knit cast that loved a good session of real talk, but we were also all busy, stressed, and wrapped up in our own lives. Hindsight is twenty-twenty.

Cory's gone, and I miss him, and that is what it is. The only consolation I have is that I've always trusted that God has a plan for me, and he must have had one for Cory too, even if I don't understand it.

GLEEFUL AND GRATEFUL

I recently went back and started watching old episodes from the beginning, and I'm proud to say that a lot of them made me laugh out loud. And as soap-operatic and after school-specialish as some of the plot lines were, there were also a lot of truisms in the show, like when Santana declares, "Life is very high school, just with bigger stakes."

If I had a dollar for every time my mom reminded me that God had a plan, I'd probably use them to buy a new Prada bag. But, point being, I didn't always believe her, especially in some of the harder moments, when I was broke and hadn't booked a role in years. Even when I was up for something that I didn't really think I wanted, I'd be devastated when I didn't get it, crying at the kitchen table about how I was doomed to just be a Hooters waitress for the rest of my life.

She'd just shake her head and tell me not to worry, that if God was shutting some doors, it was so I'd pay attention to the ones that were open. And she was right. If I'd gotten even just one of the roles I had thought I wanted, I might never have auditioned for *Glee*. And that's where I truly believe I was destined to end up.

It would be an understatement to say that *Glee* changed my life. It overhauled it. It got me out of debt. It helped to cement my career. And before the show, I'd never had a group of people I was that close with. I think a lot of the other cast members would say the same thing (except, maybe not about the debt . . .). But while *Glee* changed our lives, it didn't necessarily change who we were. We started the show as a ragtag group of misfits, and six seasons later, when we filmed the last episode, we were still the same bunch of misfits. Just now wearing more expensive jeans.

SORRY:

- *Cory passing. Nothing was ever the same without him.*

- *The crunchy ringlet curls in my ponytail from seasons one to three.*

- *What felt like day 12,157 in a cheerleading uniform.*

NOT SORRY:

- *Working hard and playing even harder.*

- *All the lifelong friendships I made: Heather, Chris, Amber, Dianna, Kevin, Jenna, Harry, Telly, and too many more to name all of them here.*

- *Playing Santana Lopez—a character who meant so much to so many people—and watching her grow up on-screen while I grew up offscreen.*

- *Spending six years dancing, singing, and working my ass off as part of something memorable and amazing.*

FROM BOYS TO MEN
Learning the Difference Between Lust and Love

M Y FIRST CRUSH was Bel Biv DeVoe. Not one
in particular, but all of them. One of my mom's
friends had given me a BBD tape as a present at
my fifth-birthday party at Chuck E. Cheese's. It
was in no way an appropriate gift for a kindergartner, but I
was instantly obsessed. I watched their videos and fell in
l-o-v-e. I had an inkling that this was possibly inappropriate,
so I'd only listen to their songs in my room and imitate the
grinding dance moves by myself in front of the mirror.

Once, my parents and I ran into DeVoe in the mall. My
dad, knowing I was a fan, picked me up and took me over to
say hi. I was too embarrassed to even make eye contact,
though, and as they chatted it up, I buried my head in my
dad's shoulder and snuck secret glances at DeVoe, all the

while thinking, "I have sexy dreams about you, and in them we're living together!"

I also definitely remember refusing to nap at preschool, preferring to stay wide awake and chase boys around the playroom. I don't think I was particularly boy crazy—I think I just wanted what a lot of girls want, which is a boyfriend, but I guess maybe I've just wanted one since I was a toddler.

Since things never worked out with me and DeVoe, my next crush was more attainable, and age appropriate: Tahj Mowry, Tia and Tamera's little brother. Tahj and I did a print shoot together when we were four. Our moms became friends on set, and, soon after, my family started attending the same church as them. After a few years of seeing each other every Sunday morning, Tahj was my number one crush, and I suspect that I was his.

Tahj had made several appearances on *Sister, Sister*, but when we were preteens, he was cast to star in his own WB show, *Smart Guy*, playing a child genius who skips ahead six grades and into high school. When my thirteenth-birthday party rolled around, I told all the girls at school that Tahj was going to be there, and the reaction was akin to what you would expect if Channing Tatum made a surprise appearance at a bachelorette party. Tahj showed up a little bit late, at which point his arrival had been thoroughly hyped, and every female at the party, sans me, freaked out. Bitches were *thirsty*, immediately decamping to corners and whispering and giggling at one another. We had a basketball hoop in the backyard, and when Tahj said he wanted to play, all the girls did too.

There wasn't a one of them who could throw a ball even anywhere near the basket, but this didn't stop them all from thronging the court. It was nonstop double dribbles and air balls until one of them would "accidentally" brush up against Tahj and then run off the court screaming, "I touched him, I touched him!" Some hair was going to get pulled if they didn't stop rushing up on my man, but a disaster was averted when we slow danced in front of everyone, including our moms—er, when our moms made us slow dance, if I'm being totally honest here . . .

We had our first kiss not too long after that, when we were on a chaperoned date with—who else but—our moms. We'd gone to see a Denzel Washington movie, and our moms had made the mistake (or maybe it was deliberate?) of sitting in the row in front of us. This left me and Tahj free to hold hands behind their backs, and even, gasp, make out! I'd never kissed anybody before, and I'm pretty sure he hadn't either, because our teeth kept knocking together so frequently, and so loudly, that I thought one of our moms would turn around and go, "What the hell is that noise?!" Finally, we stopped attempting to kiss and just sat and quietly held hands in the dark.

After that, I considered Tahj to be my almost boyfriend, as he was certainly the closest I'd ever come to having a real boyfriend as a teenager, though we were really more like best friends. We had the same sense of humor and shared that actor's tendency to always be on, entertaining each other by dramatically resinging every song we heard on the radio and adding tons of runs. I liked that he was a nice, Christian boy, and we genuinely had fun whenever we were together, even though we rarely did more than awkwardly slobber on each other's faces and hold hands.

I was his date for his winter formal at a private school that was way fancier than Valencia High, and also even his date on the night when he was nominated for an NAACP Image Award. It was my first red carpet. I wore a white two-piece number, a matching shirt and skirt that almost could have been sexy, or at least cute, if my mom hadn't made me wear a long slip underneath it like I was a freaking Mormon.

Like something straight out of the embarrassing stories in *Seventeen* magazine, that also happened to be the day I got my period for the first time—the same day as the biggest date of my life, when I'd been planning for weeks to wear all white. My mother, bless her heart, had always explained menstruation to me as an afterthought, saying things like, "Oh well, when you get your period . . . ," as if I was somehow just supposed to know what getting my period was all about.

So that day, when I went to the bathroom and found blood in my underwear, I immediately told my mom, who just screeched, "Naya, oh my God, you're a woman now!" then handed me a pad to stick in my panties and pretty much pushed me out the door and into the limo where Tahj and his mom were waiting.

Pads are not the most technologically advanced period protection. They feel like you're wearing an XXL diaper all bunched up between your legs, especially when you've never worn one before. As I walked down the sidewalk to get into the car, I was terrified that I was waddling, and that Tahj would take one look at me and be able to immediately tell what was happening, and that, worse, he'd be totally grossed out by it. I felt like I had a secret but wasn't sure if it was a good or bad secret. "Oh my God," I wondered, as I took my seat next to him, "can he smell the blood?" But he didn't seem to notice anything, and barely even noticed me, as he spent the entire ride there practicing his acceptance speech for an award he did not win.

Tahj and I continued to "date" off and on for the entirety of our teenage years. During one of our off periods, I lost my virginity to someone else. Tahj later ended things once and for all by telling me he thought he needed to date someone more on his financial level. Dick. We're still friends.

LOSING IT

One day, toward the end of high school, it seemed like I just woke up and none of my friends were virgins anymore. Tahj and my whatever it was, was pretty much a sexless union, and there had never been anyone else who seemed worth having sex with. The senior who'd taken me to prom when I was a sophomore had tried to have sex with me that night after the dance, but I rightly turned him down. After all, he had a nose ring and was rumored to have once gotten a blow job while sitting on the toilet, taking a shit. What a prince.

Some of my friends had been doing it for a long time; others professed to like having sex but love giving BJs. They'd just be like, "What? I like it!" Whatever. I was sick of not being able to participate in these girl-talk sessions and figured it was high time to hand over my V card. But who was going to be the lucky guy? There was one thing that I did know, though—this guy was not going to be special.

As much as my friends claimed to just love having sex, I'd seen the same thing happen to all of them: they'd give it up to a guy they really liked, get dumped, and then spend the next two months blubbering and crying, "But he took my vir-gin-i-tyyyyyy! Wahhhhhhhh . . ." I was damn certain that was not going to be me.

One day not long after high school graduation I was working an afternoon shift at Abercrombie when my target came in, just shopping for sweat shirts. It was a guy I'd gone to junior high with and hadn't seen in years. He was half-white, half-black, somehow Mormon, and had morphed into a pretty hot dude since the last time I saw him, in eighth grade. "That's it," I thought. "Good enough." We exchanged numbers, and I hit him up a few days later. I don't think he had any idea what was coming (pun intended).

Mixed Mormon and I went on a few dates that weren't too bad but weren't too good either. I told my best friend, Madison, that I was going to lose my virginity.

She was shocked. "What?! Do you like him? Do you love him?"

No and no, I told her, and that was the whole point.

One night, MM was at a friend's house, playing video games, and I texted him that I was coming over. It was getting late, like nine at night, and I drove myself and parked outside. I took a deep breath before I walked in, and if I could have high-fived myself, I would have.

We hung out for a few minutes, me watching him play Grand Theft Auto, when I suggested that we go into his friend's bedroom. Maybe he was starting to catch on at this point, because he readily agreed. We made out for a few minutes, and then I pushed him down, stared him in the eyes, and said, "Okay, let's get this over with, because I don't want to bleed on someone I actually like." For a teenage boy, sweeter words of seduction have never been spoken, I guess, and then I climbed on top and proceeded to get it over with.

As soon as I was back outside and a safe distance from the house, I called Madison.

"I did it!"

"That's it?!"

"That's it!" I never talked to him again, and to this day I'm pretty proud to say that I lost my virginity on top.

THE WHORE YEARS—AND WHY EVERY GIRL NEEDS THEM

After that, Tahj and I got back together for a bit, but I still wasn't getting much action. When he dumped me, I took it as my cue, and was like, "Okay, well, I guess I'll start fucking now," and commenced what I now refer to with nothing but fond memories and affection as the "whore years." Abercrombie was a great place for hookups, because the guys all had great bodies and, well, you didn't have to go very far. You'd basically bump into someone running clothes from the fitting room and think, "Okay, you!"

After that, I set my sights on my longtime high school crush, who was a super hot, six-foot-one white boy with long hair and muscles. I'd had my eye on this guy—we'll call him A—since freshman year, but he was popular and only went out with the prettiest girls in school. He never looked at me, but now that we were out of high school (and, I'm sure, because I now had C-cups), when we ran into each other, it seemed like we were finally on the same level.

I started my long and complicated plot to get to him by dating his best friend (if you haven't picked up on it yet, this is where I started getting real whorish). His best friend was a similarly hot black dude who looked like Michael Jackson pre–plastic surgery and skin bleach. This guy—we'll call him B—and I dated for a while and would hook up at my best friend's house because I was still living at home with my dad. Madison still lived with her mom, but she was never home, so B and I would sneak away every chance we got and do it in Madison's bed. She was less than pleased about this, understandably.

"Naya," she'd say. "This is not cool. I sleep here!" She had a point.

Then all of a sudden, out of what seemed like nowhere, B dumped me, with little emotion or explanation. Well, hell hath no fury like a woman scorned, so I decided to get B back by hooking up with his other best friend, C.

Somehow none of these guys seemed to know who their best friends were banging (which I'm not sure I really believe), and the next time I saw A he asked for my number. Of course I gave it to him. This long and convoluted plan seemed to be working after all. A and I texted back and forth for a while, and by that time I was living in my own ill-fated apartment, so when he texted one night asking if he could come over, I said yes immediately. He came over, we watched TV for a little bit—as you do—and then did it, as you do. He left a short time later, and for some reason, as soon as he left, I couldn't find my keys.

That asshole was trying to steal my car!

Or so I thought. When I called him screaming about it, he had no idea what I was talking about. Who knows what A's and my future held, because after that, he totally thought I was nuts—and he had a point. I later found the keys between the cushions of the couch, and my car was still parked right where I'd left it.

I thought this was the end of my ABC adventure, and lost contact with all of them for a few weeks, until one day my cell phone started to ring when my mom was over at my apartment making lunch with me. I didn't recognize the number, so I just hit "answer" and put it on speaker phone.

"Hello?"

"Hi," said a male voice. "Can I speak to the coach of the all-star team?"

"What?"

"Can I speak to the coach of the all-star team? I heard you're holding tryouts for new members."

It began to dawn on me who was on the other end of the line and what was happening, and I hung up as quickly as I could. My mom was sitting there, just looking at me like, what the fuck just happened?

I had no choice but to tell her. This was right after she'd divorced my dad and was dating for the first time in almost twenty years, and we were really close. When I finished my story with "I'm really sorry I'm such a slut," she started cracking up.

Before I could stop her, she grabbed the phone from me and hit the callback button. "Hello?" she said, in her most sassy voice, as soon as the same guy who had just called me picked up. "No, this is the coach of the all-star team! And we are *not* accepting new members!" Then she hung up. By this point, she was laughing so hard that she had tears in her eyes, and I had crumpled over on the couch, unable to breathe.

My mom has had my back from day one, and nothing's going to change that, certainly not a little sleeping around.

Now I look back on my whore years and think everyone should have them. I don't think you can be successfully married until you've had at least three good years of playing the field. I'm not kidding! It teaches you what's out there (even if it's not all that great) so you'll know good sex when you find it later. You'll learn how to get yourself off, get other people off, and how to get other people to get you off. You'll learn to not shed tears for the d-bags; sleep with a few people who you might really care about, even if you don't want them to be your boyfriend (or girlfriend); and learn that being a woman and having sex isn't about just "giving it up" but getting yours too.

And, fuck, it's fun. You get some great stories in the process. Years from now, when I'm still married and Ryan and I have all these kids and grandkids running around, I can sit back and think, "Yeah, I lived. I really lived."

RELATIONSHIP TERRITORY—IT'S COMPLICATED

After Tahj and my sexless teenage union was officially donezo—and you're definitely over-over when someone breaks up with you because your family's poor—I went on dates and had hookups, but there was nothing really memorable or remarkable about any of the guys I hung out with. Or wait, let me rephrase that: memorable in a *good* way.

I dated this one guy for a while, an actor who'd shown some career promise after a small role in a movie, and he was a couple of years younger than me. He was legal but still didn't have a car or even a driver's license. His mom drove him everywhere. We'd hang out, hook up, and then when it was time for him to go, I'd drive him to some halfway point, like a McDonald's parking lot, where his mom would be waiting. He'd give me a kiss, get out of my car, walk across the parking lot, and get in her car; then she'd wave and they'd drive off. It was like two divorced parents with joint custody, and it only took me a couple of times meeting his mom at the drop-off point before I was like, yeah, this is probably not going to work.

My string of randoms came to an end when I met Mark Salling at the *Glee* pilot. He played guitar and I thought he was so cute. This was Mark Salling circa 2009, when he was still a major looker, and I tried so hard to get him to like me. At the time, I still wasn't sure how long my role on *Glee* would last, so I was still working as a nanny on the side in order to make some extra money. My phone rang one day while I was working. I was standing there, surrounded by all these kids, when I answered this unknown number (probably assuming that it was yet another credit agency). But it was Mark, wanting to know if I wanted to go out. On a date. With him.

Of course I did.

It was October, right before Halloween, and we made plans to go to Fright Fest at Magic Mountain, even though I normally hate that kind of stuff and don't like to be scared at all. Like I said, I was trying so hard to get him to like me. I still had my bad hair extensions at this point, but I spent extra time straightening them and putting on makeup, and I wore a white American Apparel V-neck tee and a plaid flannel shirt tied around my waist—a casual autumnal Fright Fest outfit, I thought. Mark came to pick me up, and he was driving a complete piece-of-shit car with trash just rolling around in the backseat. Okay, I could forgive him that—we were all still struggling at that point. I don't even remember what kind of car it was, so I think I must have blocked it out.

It's harder to block the fact that he then proceeded to smoke weed in front of me, even when I declined his offer to get high, but, like I said, he was smoking hot at that point, so I just focused on his biceps and tried to ignore the cloud of marijuana smoke billowing around my head. As soon as he was done, he asked if I was hungry. I said yes, thinking, "Oh my God, we're going to dinner! This is so cute!"

Then he pulled into the In-N-Out drive-through, the one nearest my house, still in Valencia. As we ordered, I kept telling myself that this date was going well. "I'm a down chick," I thought. "I can eat a cheeseburger." Which I did, sitting in the car in the parking lot. When we'd finished our meal, it took a few tries before we got the car to start, but at least the smell of weed had been replaced by the smell of fries.

At Fright Fest, Mark was very high and very excited. He loved all the ghouls and monsters, and had even brought a camera—not to take pictures of me, or the two of us, but to get pics of himself with all the different people in costume. It was pretty weird, and I wish I had those photos, because if I did, they would definitely be in this book. All in all, though, the date was not a total disaster, and we ended it with nothing more than a friendly hug.

A few weeks later, we kissed for the first time on the night that Obama was elected. I was watching the election results at home in Valencia with my dad, and when it looked like Obama really was going to win, I was totally overcome with patriotism and excitement and called Mark. "What are you doing right now?"

He was celebrating at a bar in Santa Monica and was as enthusiastic as I was. "Come and meet me!" he yelled into the phone. "I'm coming!" I yelled back.

Once we met up, we got drunk and made out, periodically taking breaks to yell, "Can you believe this?" or "Yes, we can!" and wipe tears of joy from our eyes. Then I spent the night at his house. After that, we somehow became boyfriend and girlfriend, and he told me he loved me just four weeks into us hanging out. This time he wasn't high on weed or political progress, but ecstasy.

We were about to go out, when he pulled out this pill and asked if I wanted to do it with him. At first I said no, because I'd never done ecstasy before, but he finally convinced me to split it with him. As soon as I was done, he turned to me and said, "Hey, so I'm just going to say this now because I'm probably going to say it later, but I love you." Then the car pulled up, and off we went, before I even had time to really decide what to say back. "Do I say that I love him?" I wondered. "No, because I don't." I was also intensely examining every emotion and physical feeling for some sign that the drug might be working. But it wasn't, and I still didn't know what to say, so finally I just said, "Thank you?" We went to the Happy Ending on Sunset, and Mark spent the entire night high as a kite, smiling his ass off, and I never felt a thing. Except maybe a vague sense of paranoia and impending doom, but that might just be in hindsight.

Mark and I went on to date for three years. During that time, we were either very much on or very much off, but he was my first real boyfriend. Woof. When things were good, they were great. He was from Texas, and I went home with him twice. Texas might as well have been a whole new world, through the eyes of a California girl, but I loved it. We went to visit his grandma and stayed, just the two of us, at his family's creek-side cabin. He'd play the guitar and we'd lay in the sun and write songs and go fishing. We were that fucking retarded couple, where I'd be like, "Oh, baby, you caught me a bass!"

Glee was a new experience for both of us, so it was great to have a buddy to get through all the shit with, and being on set together was really fun—when we weren't hating each other.

Because Mark was one of the leads in the show, people started to recognize him long before they knew who I was. His star was on the rise—at least to hear him tell it—and so he explained to me the deal: his publicist thought it would be better for his image if he pretended to not have a girl-friend. "If anyone asks," he said, "I'm single." Fine, whatever. I agreed to that, though I had a feeling his pretending to be single had less to do with his publicist and more to do with his dick. A saner woman would have walked away from that relationship right then and there, but two things stopped me from doing so: one, I was not a sane woman at that time in my life, and two, to break up with Mark would mean I wouldn't have a reason to fight with him anymore. And I loved fighting with him. I was addicted to the drama.

He's a moody fucking person, and whenever he'd get in a mood, I'd start feeling some type of way. I'd do something to push his buttons, which would make him withdraw even more and piss me off even more. I was constantly asking him if there were other girls—which, let's be honest, there totally were—but he would deny it, and then I'd demand to see his phone, and when he'd refuse, I'd try to get sneaky and grab it the second he let his guard down. All in the name of good, clean, unhealthy fun!

The POS car he drove when we first started dating was pretty indicative of what Mark was like—there were a lot of areas of his life where he just did not give a fuck. Where he lived was another one of them. He had this apartment in a sketchy neighborhood. It was right next to a liquor store, the next-door neighbor's door was riddled with bullet holes, and if I ever had to park more than just a few feet away from his place, I'd lock my car and then run as quickly as I could. One time we even came home and found that a homeless person had taken a giant shit right on his welcome mat. But Mark didn't care one bit, and didn't even move out of that place until season three.

But still, I was in love, or so I thought, and I'd be sleeping over at that shithole apartment, happy as a lark, thinking, "I could live here if we were married. I could definitely fix it up." Oh, to be young and completely deranged.

Once, he was away on a trip, and word came back to me through other members of the cast that he had fucked some other girl. I'd always suspected such things had happened, but this was the first time someone had flat-out said to me, "Yo, he banged that chick," so I instantly was pissed.

I called up Madison, my forever partner in crime, and we drove down to Mark's apartment while he was still out of town. We made a pit stop at the liquor store next door and bought dog food, Coca-Cola, eggs, and bird seed, and then dumped all that shit all over his car. I took video of it. He was still scheduled to be gone for a few more days, but by the time we were pulling away the feral cats had already started to come mewing out of the alley and were jumping up onto the car to eat the food.

And that's how I got my first media scandal. A sample headline from *Us Weekly*: "Exclusive: *Glee*'s Naya Rivera Keyed Mark Salling's Lexus in Jealous Fit." Someone leaked it to the press but got all the details wrong—there were no keys involved, and he definitely did not have a Lexus. I never fully admitted it to anyone, but Mark knew it was me. He was friendly with the people who ran the liquor store, and when he got back to find his car covered in fermenting sludge, they showed him surveillance-camera footage of me in the store, buying all the stuff. Whoops.

Mark might have had a shred of guilt about sleeping around behind my back, or—more likely—he was as addicted to the drama as I was, because we kept at it, even after this incident. He even helped me cover it up, and we posted a pic to his Twitter account of me pretending to choke him while wearing my Cheerios uniform. "I don't even drive a Lexus. Silly rumors, we're the best of friends," he captioned the photo, and we never talked about it again.

We continued to bicker and break up every other day, and then finally Mark had had enough. He ended it for good, against my wishes. For a while, there was drama on set, because we hated each other and I didn't even want him looking at me. Any time a new person was added to the show, it was like fresh meat being dropped into a piranha tank. Eyebrows went up and hormones started churning at the thought of new hookup potential. Lucky for me, Chord Overstreet joined the cast right after Mark and I were donezo, and the minute I saw him it was like a lightbulb went off. "You don't know my drama with Mark," I thought. "Hey," I said to Chord, "let's hang out!"

Of course, it didn't take long at all for word of said drama to reach Chord, and he confronted me on set one day, while at the same time trying to hide from Mark. "But I'm friends with him!" Chord protested, before ducking behind a car as Mark just happened to walk by. "Don't let him see me!" Chord hissed from his crouch.

Within a few weeks, though, I was like, "Mark who?" and Chord was like, "Naya who?" and everyone had completely forgotten about it and moved on. That was one of many good things about the *Glee* cast—it was impossible to stay mad for long; we knew how to keep it moving.

So what did I learn from that completely dysfunctional relationship? Nothing. Absolutely nothing—until Mark's legal woes (google it) made a few unsavory headlines on their own a few years later. My son's nanny actually told me about it when the story broke. I can't say I was totally shocked, but still—W-T-F? Then I had no doubt that God really did have my back along the way. When Mark dumped me, I thought it was the worst thing ever, but can you imagine if that didn't happen? And I was laying there in bed when the battering ram came through the door? (Again, google it!)

Similar to how I feel about the whore years, I think everyone should have that one relationship where you look back and ask yourself, "What the hell was I thinking?" You'll learn something and you won't regret it. Unless, of course, that relationship was with someone who had a sizable stash of child porn on his computer. Then, by all means, regret everything.

BUMP IN THE ROAD

One of the reasons why I don't (totally) regret what happened between Mark and me is that, had this shitty relationship never happened, I might never have met my husband.

It was 2010 and, as was often the case in those days, I was in a horrible mood because of Mark. It was either a break, breakup, or fight (hard to keep track), but I had plans to sit at home and wait for him to call me so I could scream that I never wanted to talk to him again and hang up. Heather had no intention of letting this happen, though, and told me that I was coming out that night if she had to come by my house and pick me up. I conceded that she was probably right, and agreed to meet her at a burlesque show in Santa Monica, where one of our dancer friends was going to be performing.

Almost as soon as we walked into the club, I noticed Ryan sitting at the bar. It was a classic double take, like something out of a movie, my head swiveling around on my neck and my eyes practically popping out of my head. He had a chiseled jaw, long curly hair, and a black bandanna tied around his head. "Who is that?" I asked Heather, and when I wouldn't stop talking about him, she decided to go find out for me.

Heather walked up to him, pointed me out, and said something along the lines of "My friend thinks you're cute and wants to talk to you."

And what did Ryan say? He wasn't having it. "I like things to happen organically," he told Heather (as a polite way of saying no), and she came back to our table alone. I couldn't believe it! I do not take no for an answer, so I spent the next forty-five minutes pounding drinks to get up the courage to go talk to him myself. Finally, I walked over and introduced myself. "Hi, I'm Naya," I said. "How are you liking it?"

He asked, how was he liking what? The show, I told him, and he laughed and shrugged, saying it was okay. That conversation topic exhausted, I was like, "Well, I just want to say congratulations."

"On what?"

"On your incredible bone structure."

"It's just the lighting," he insisted, but my blatant pickup line must not have been that bad, because he asked me to sit down. We spent the rest of the night just talking, and I remember his body language never changed at all. He never seemed very receptive, and I had total flashbacks to chasing boyfriends in preschool. At the end of the night, though, we exchanged info.

"We should be friends," he said, as he punched his number into my phone.

"Great," I said, "I love friends." That was a total lie, because friends was not exactly what I was going for.

Later, after we'd known each other for a while, he told me that he'd had no idea who I was, but that his friends had recognized me from the show. "That's that girl from *Glee*," one of them told him on the way home. "You must be something if she wants to talk to you."

"Yeah?" he said. "It's cool, we're friends." And after that, we were friends. For about five minutes.

Our first date was at the bowling alley Pinz on Ventura. Now, the way dates had always seemed to work for me was that I would meet some guy at a bar or a club or through friends and we'd make plans to hang out one-on-one. Then he'd show up and be nowhere near as hot as I remembered him (I guess this is what people call beer goggles, huh?). But with Ryan, it was the total opposite: he was even better looking than I had expected, wearing a tank top that showed off his wiry muscles, and another black bandanna tied around his head. We went bowling and played arcade games. It was *that* kind of date, and I laughed all night and had a really good time.

At the end of the night, I followed him back to his house. We hung out in his backyard, where he built a little bonfire in the grass. We were sitting there, him smoking a joint and me smoking a cigarette, when suddenly he leaned over and tried to kiss me.

"What are you doing?" I gasped, determined to now play hard to get with the guy I'd been pursuing. He apologized, and we sat there being friends for the next twenty minutes, before I thought, "What the hell," and leaned over and kissed him. We made out that night, and then were inseparable for the next three months.

Because of his long hair, my friends and I called him Tarzan, and they all loved him. Telly had an annual "pink and cheap" party, where the gist of the evening was that everyone came wearing pink and looking cheap—duh. Ryan wore a pink suit, and I dressed like an angel, wearing cheap wings and a whore skirt to complement my hair extensions. I had no idea why Ryan liked me, because I might have had the wings on but he was the angel.

He would come over and cook me dinner, and whenever we were together, I always had the best time. I'd never been so comfortable with anyone, and he treated me so well. Once I was really sick with strep and missed a day and a half of work (you had to be practically on your deathbed to call in sick at *Glee*), and when I woke up, Ryan had somehow snuck past the gate of my apartment complex and left a bouquet of Winnie-the-Pooh balloons and a portable cooler full of popsicles on my front porch. He didn't even wake me up.

So of course I had to break up with him. I'd never had a guy treat me so well, so I assumed there had to be something wrong with him, something major that would only come out later. Why else would he want to be with me? I was young and stupid at the time, and my role on *Glee* was just starting to take off. I needed to focus on my career and didn't need any dream killer around to mess it up. I was going to keep it moving.

I told him all this one night over the phone, as I sat in my bathrobe in my apartment. I explained that no, I didn't really have a good reason for breaking up with him, and no, we weren't going to discuss it. "I don't want to talk to you anymore," I said, and then he said something that stuck in my head, verbatim, for years.

"Wow, Naya, you're a fucked-up kid." Then he hung up, and that was that.

The next day I went to work and told everyone, assuming they'd be excited, because everyone loved drama and a good breakup story. Instead, they were aghast.

"Why?! What's wrong with you? He was really cool." The consensus seemed to be that Ryan was right—I really was a fucked-up kid—but too late now. Tarzan was gone.

A few weeks later we were shooting the wedding episode of *Glee*, and when we wrapped, we went out to dinner as a cast. Everyone kept commenting on how great my tits had looked in my bridesmaid's dress. No big deal, because, like I said, it was just that kind of work environment—i.e., an inappropriate one. I didn't think much of it.

When I got back to my loft later, I randomly decided to piss on this stick—a.k.a. a pregnancy test. I don't even remember why exactly I decided to do it, except for the fact that I did it all the time. I had been terrified of getting pregnant my whole life (probably that old dream-killer thing, and the fact that it had happened to my mom), and taking a pregnancy test was practically a weekly ritual for me, not really to see if I was pregnant but more to prove to myself that I wasn't.

Except this time, holy fuck! It was eleven at night, and when I took the pregnancy test, it turned out positive. The last person I'd had sex with was Ryan, and we were always carefulish, and so this didn't make any sense. Immediately, I jumped into my car and drove to a twenty-four hour CVS, where I proceeded to buy one of every brand and type of pregnancy test they had available.

Back at my apartment, I just sat on the toilet, chugging water and peeing on all of them, then lining them up along the sink, one by one, as they all came out positive. Finally, after about six of them, I had no remaining doubt. I knew I was pregnant.

Hysterically crying, I called my mom and woke her up. It was now almost one in the morning. "I'm pregnant, and it's Tarzan's baby!"

"What?" she said, waking up. "What have you been doing?"

I had no idea; I hadn't been doing anything out of the ordinary, and had even been extra responsible—I thought—by breaking off this relationship so I could put my career first. Plus, accidentally getting pregnant had always been a phobia of mine, and now it was coming true. It felt surreal, and I sobbed into the phone.

Finally, my mom told me to calm down, get some rest, and that she would make some calls the next day. I got in bed and cried myself to sleep, tossing fitfully for a few hours before my 7:00 a.m. call time. At work I put my cheerleading uniform on carefully, feeling like there was an alien taking over my body, and wondered what I was going to do. I couldn't even get off work to go to the dentist.

From the minute I made that first phone call to my mom, it was never a question of whether I was going to have the baby. I just knew I couldn't. And without even saying it, my mom knew it too. It made it easier, because I felt like I never had to question if I was making the right decision, but, still, nothing about the next few weeks was even remotely easy.

At the time, I didn't even have a regular gynecologist, so step one was making a doctor's appointment to confirm that I actually was pregnant, and if so, how far along. It turned out I was four weeks along. I had to start then and there going to my bosses and trying to get time off. I begged and begged Brad, who assured me that we were already behind on shooting and there was no way they could accommodate me being gone for even one day. There was nothing more stressful than working on *Glee* and having to deal with any kind of personal issue, because it was an extreme case of "the show must go on." I finally told him I had a medical emergency of the female kind, which was the truth, and he agreed to let me have one day. One day, and that one day was still two weeks off.

Those two weeks were excruciating. I was so stressed out that I could barely eat, and smoking was the only thing that calmed me down, even though it also made me feel guilty, because I'd wonder if it was okay. Everything about it was fucked up. In retrospect, I think the fact that it was a logistical nightmare was actually something of a saving grace, as it kept me from having to deal with the emotional nightmare of it.

As you can probably imagine, whether to have an abortion is about the most personal, complicated decision a woman can ever have to make, and I was terrified that someone would see me, recognize me, or leak my story to the press.

Finally, my day off rolled around. My mom picked me up, and we drove to a Planned Parenthood center in Pasadena, figuring it was far enough away from Hollywood and our own community that the chances of seeing anyone we knew, or anyone who knew me, would be pretty low. Mom and I had gone wig shopping a few days before, and we drove to the appointment with me in a horrific black Florence Henderson wig with red tips, an oversize hoodie, sunglasses, and baggy jeans. We paid cash, leaving no paper trail, like it was a drug deal, and my mom waited in the lobby for me, for two hours, while I slept in the car outside. My mother is a saint, and the most badass woman I know.

After what felt like forever, it was my turn. I had opted to take the abortion pill, as opposed to having a surgical procedure, which meant I took the first pill in the office and the second one at home several hours later. I took it at my mom's house, lying on the couch, and it was the worst experience of my life. It was incredibly painful—your body is basically in labor with strong, frequent contractions. I was nauseated and kept going in and out of consciousness because of the pain.

After the worst of it was over, I continued to bleed for about two and a half weeks, which meant that when I got up to work the next day, a little more than twelve hours after having a medical abortion, I had to put my cheerleading uniform back on and hope that the skimpy bloomers covered the giant pad I was wearing.

I never told Ryan about any of this.

Over the years, he would e-mail me, and I didn't write back. He'd get in touch with some of my friends here and there, and they'd always be like, "Why don't you date Tarzan again? He was always so nice!" But they didn't know and I couldn't tell them. I was afraid to talk to Ryan again, because I didn't know where to start.

Anyone who's familiar with Los Angeles knows it's hardly a place where you just run into people—you can go years without running into your next-door neighbor—and I'd never run into anyone I'd dated. Except for Ryan, more than two years after we'd last spoken, and at a car wash of all places. I gave him my e-mail, and we started hanging out again. Though tentatively, because he was soon moving to New York indefinitely. When we were together, I felt like I had no control over my mouth. I'd open it, and some pointed question would come falling out: "So, do you think you've ever gotten anyone pregnant? If you and I had a kid, what do you think it would look like?"

It was my subconscious taking control and trying to trick him into asking what I was talking about, but Ryan never took the bait. The night before he left for New York, we made out in the car, and I told him that if things were different I would marry him and have his babies. And before we said good-bye, I said, "Come back for me" as dramatically as if I were Kate Winslet going down with the ship. A year later, he did—he sent me an e-mail when he moved back to LA. I had just started dating someone else, and not knowing what to write back, I never responded.

Ironically enough, though I never told Ryan about the abortion, I told every other guy I dated after that. It became something I fixated on, and it snowballed inside me to the point where I felt that if someone was going to date me, he should understand what I was dealing with.

I'd think about it frequently, sometimes fixating on it so much that I'd give myself a near panic attack, and then call my mom, sobbing. I was so angry at myself, and I felt I should have weighed my options more. Why was I so career driven that I just automatically assumed I couldn't have a kid at twenty-three? I started to resent work—I felt like they didn't care about us and owed me for what I'd had to do, even though they'd had no idea.

Some of the triggers that got me thinking about my abortion were obvious things, like thinking about Ryan, but there were also triggers that seemed to come out of nowhere. I became addicted to *Teen Mom*, and it was my favorite show because I was so jealous that they got to keep their kids. Watching it over and over was a way of punishing myself. "What's wrong with you?" I'd ask myself. "These people have no money and they kept their child. You could have supported a kid."

I don't think I ever emotionally healed from the abortion, which is why it is so mind-blowing that some people think having an abortion is the carefree girl's number one choice to keep on partying. In reality, it is anything but an easy choice. In some ways, I think choosing to have an abortion is almost harder than choosing to have your child, because you make that choice knowing, or at least suspecting, that many moments of your life will now be tinged with regret. I don't think I processed my abortion until I was pregnant with Ryan's child again—this time when we were married and the baby was planned. This was when I finally felt like God's plan for us had come full circle. Long before we were even together, Ryan had thought for years about what he'd want to name a kid, and when we talked about that name and looked into it more, one of its meanings was "God shall add a second son." It seemed predestined. I don't want it to seem like I "chose" this child over the other; it was just that this time I felt ready. That's all I can say, and the only way I can explain it.

Abortion will always be a very controversial subject, and I thought a lot about whether I wanted to share my story in this book. I know that I'll be judged for it, and that no matter how hard I try to explain how I felt and my reasons for doing it, a lot of people won't understand. I ultimately decided I wanted to share it because I'm not the only one with this experience. Approximately three in ten women in the United States will have an abortion by the time they are forty-five. Yet a lot of those women will go through it alone, or at least thinking they're alone.

About a week before I was supposed to give birth to my son, Ryan and I went out to dinner. I got up to go to the bathroom—as you do a lot when you're nine months pregnant—and walked in on two girls in the restaurant's tiny, one-stall bathroom. They were bad-girl clubbing it, totally drunk and smelling like cigarettes. They were taking selfies in the mirror, but when one of them saw me, she turned around and looked me up and down.

"I just had an abortion," she slurred. "How sad is that?"

Her friend's jaw dropped, but the girl continued, telling me her story and repeating over and over, "Isn't that the saddest thing?"

I didn't know what to say, so I kept nodding and finally said, "I totally get it. That is a really difficult thing to have to go through." But I wanted to be like, "You're not alone! Wait until my book comes out!" I also recognized a part of myself in her—in the way she almost couldn't keep the story in, in how she opened her mouth and just poured out her heart to a complete stranger. That was how I had felt with all the guys I had dated after Ryan: telling them was almost a physical need, something I felt compelled to do. Having an abortion is a secret that gets bigger the longer you keep it in.

And excuse me for stepping into high school sex-ed teacher mode here for a minute, but I think it's important—there's no award for best effort when it comes to safe sex. If you practice safe sex 95 percent of the time, you don't get an A—you get an F. All it takes is one time to get pregnant. I thought that as long as I was pretty cautious, I'd be fine, and that was wrong. A lot of times, the idea of practicing safe sex, and especially talking about it, seems completely unsexy. Understandable. But you know what's really unsexy? An abortion. So while I make light about things like the whore years and gaining sexual experience, it's incredibly important to be responsible while you're exploring.

Had Ryan and I been as careful as we should have been, we could have saved ourselves a whole lot of hurt. Having an

FROM BOYS TO MEN

abortion was the most traumatic experience of my life, and I did it when I was an adult, and with my mom by my side as an incredible pillar of support. She held my hand, both literally and metaphorically, throughout the entire process and made sure I knew that I was unconditionally loved by her and by God. And it was still fucking hard. I can't imagine how it feels to be a teenager who goes through something like that and then has to head back to the halls of high school, or to be a woman who feels she can't even tell the people she's closest to.

It's just such a personal decision, based on so many factors, including where you are in your life at the time and how you feel about everything from parenting to finances and family. The sad thing is that many women who find themselves suddenly facing an unplanned pregnancy will be judged no matter what it is they decide to do. Young, single mom? Judged. Abortion? Judged. There's no way to win, to make a decision that feels wholly right.

I think every woman should have the right to choose, and it scares me to think of a world where the decision of whether to have a child is not her choice to make. I feel like I've found more ways to cope now, and I'm as at peace with my decision as I ever will be, but I still wouldn't wish an abortion on anybody, ever.

When I finally told Ryan, more than four years after it had happened, I told him that I thought there was a reason he kept coming back into my life, and that I had something important I needed to tell him. But first—I made him sign a confidentiality agreement. This sounds like a dick move, but

I was scared. I didn't know how he would react, and if he was incredibly angry that I hadn't told him before, I wouldn't have blamed him.

He was obviously confused, but was like, "Fine, I'll sign whatever you want." When I'd finished telling him, he didn't say anything, and just got up and walked away. We were at my house, and he went and stood outside on the balcony. I wanted to give him some time to process it, so I didn't follow. A few minutes later, he came back in, and said the best thing anyone could have ever said in that situation.

"In the three short months that we dated," he said, "I wish I would have done something better, to make you feel like you could have trusted me with that information, because I would have loved to be there for you."

That night, Ryan stayed over, and we've been together ever since.

SORRY:

- *Deciding to have an abortion. This was the most painful experience of my life.*

- *Not being more careful about safe sex in the first place. It only takes one instance of getting caught up in the moment to change your life forever.*

- *Breaking up with Ryan, because I didn't recognize a good thing when I saw it.*

- *Trashing Mark Salling's car. Not that he didn't deserve it, but it wasn't the classiest thing I've ever done.*

- *For roping Madison into helping me trash Mark's car (though I know she secretly enjoyed it).*

NOT SORRY:

- *Holding on to my virginity until after high school, and then losing it on my terms.*

- *The whore years. Now I know what's out there—and, trust me, it's not much.*

- *That I could share good and bad experiences with my mom, and knowing she has my back through it all.*

- *Sharing my story. I know I'll be judged for it, but if I'm able to help even one girl in a similar situation feel less alone—then bring it on.*

- *Finally falling in love. With the right guy.*

- *Getting a second chance at parenthood with the person I was always meant to be a parent with.*

THE BEST WORST
YEAR EVER
Learning to Weather the Storms

AVE YOU EVER heard of Saturn's return? I first
learned about it on set, from Jenna Ushkowitz,
who talked about it a lot during the year she
turned twenty-eight. Saturn's return is an astro-
logical concept that basically says that in your late twenties,
when the planet Saturn completes an orbit around the sun,
it bitch-slaps you and turns your life into a total shit show.
It's not fun, but if you can ride it out and not lose your mind,
then there is a light at the end of the tunnel—clarity. At least
that's how it worked for me, thank God.

To rewind a bit.

I met my ex-fiancé, a.k.a. Big Sean, on Twitter. I know, I
know—so 2013 of us, right? While filming *Glee*, I was bored
on set one day and tweeted something about a song of his. I

didn't even really know anything about him; I just liked his music, so I didn't think much about it.

Then later that day, he DM'd me—"Thanks, lady. I'm a big fan of yours too, keep up the good work." Whoa, I thought, he watches *Glee*? I was sitting with Lea between takes, and I read her the message.

"Oh my God," I said, "am I going to date this rapper?"

She shrugged—"Maybe?" And then sure enough, that was exactly what happened.

Sean was on an international tour at the time, so we started talking on Twitter, and after I gave him my number, texting. Soon, we progressed to real-live phone calls. I was living in Beverly Hills at the time, and my house was this weird black hole with no cell reception. Lucy, my dog, got a lot of walks in those days, because the park was the only place where my phone seemed to work.

He'd call me whenever he had downtime, and we cycled through all the normal getting-to-know-you topics: music, work, family, friends. Every once in a while, he'd try to be slutty, but I always shut him down real fast.

"Oh, you're going to spin class? You must know how to ride."

"This is going nowhere if you keep talking like that," I'd threaten.

Even before we'd met in person, I was really excited about it. It was fun to tell people who I was talking to—they'd always freak out: "The rapper? No way!!"

The day he finally got back into town, he called me and asked me to go to dinner. A real date—I liked that. We went to Dominick's on Beverly, and he pulled up in a white Mercedes.

Sean was a few years younger than me, but he seemed mature from the beginning. I remember thinking it was really classy that he had a Goyard wallet. I had a Goyard suitcase, and I thought, "That's a different kind of rapper. Most rappers just know about Louis Vuitton." I liked how he wasn't super flashy, and the conversation flowed well through dinner. His mom was an English teacher, and he was smart and articulate, and it felt like we had a lot in common—we were even born in the same hospital in Santa Monica. When he talked about getting signed, it was cool to see that he was as passionate as I was about making it. He also didn't seem like one of those guys who's just into hearing himself talk—he actually asked me questions too, and really listened when I told stories.

At the end of the night, as we stood outside waiting for the valet to bring our cars around, he asked me if I wanted to come over—tomorrow. Whoa! One, he wasn't trying to sleep with me on the first date, and two, we already had a second date scheduled. Cheers to that. The next day, I took him up on his offer and went over to his house. We watched Netflix, made out, and I spent the night.

Then I woke up in a panic at 6:00 a.m. It was like one of those cartoon wake-ups where your eyes pop open, and you gasp and bolt upright in bed. Had I really just spent the night with a rapper? Rap ho was not the look I was going for, so with my shoes in my hand, I snuck out of his house while he was still asleep. There was a marathon in Los

Angeles that day—streets were closed and traffic was re-routed in all kinds of directions—and I remember thinking that I was never going to get home. Not only had I made a terrible mistake, but I was also going to die in my car on Sunset Boulevard, barefoot and gasping for water. As I always did in those kinds of situations, I called my mom to talk me off the ledge.

I honestly thought I was never going to hear from him again, but I'd barely gotten home when he called me and asked me to come to his birthday party. It was the next night, and I had nothing to wear. I bought a brand-new Maison Martin Margiela jumpsuit, and they had to fly my size in from New York. The party was at Wolfgang's Steakhouse in Beverly Hills, and Sean's whole family had come in from Detroit for the occasion. I went alone, and took a deep breath as I walked in the door. There were all kinds of people there whom I recognized, like Wiz Khalifa and Jhené Aiko.

I found Sean, wished him a happy birthday, and asked where I was sitting. As I scanned the room, I wondered how many of these other girls he was hooking up with and how much work it had taken to make sure we were all seated at different tables.

"Oh," he said, "you're next to me." I choked on my champagne. Next to him meant the inner-circle table. What's more, I was right across from his mom. I imagined her asking me how I knew her son.

"Well," I'd say, "we met on Twitter and hooked up two nights ago." I downed the rest of my glass.

I didn't need to worry, though, as dinner wasn't awkward

at all. His mom turned out to be really into alternative medicine, and we talked about colonics the whole night. Neither one of us was the kind of person who finds talking about colonics awkward, and I even promised to hook her up with my girl the next time she was in town.

It was only a day or two later that Sean had to do a radio interview with Power 106 in Los Angeles. The DJ was teasing him, asking him who was the hottest girl he'd ever been with. I was driving down the freeway at the time, listening because he'd told me about it, and when he didn't miss a beat and immediately said, "Naya," I almost wrecked my car. I remember looking at the lady in the car next to me and wondering, "Does she know what just happened?"

Well, if Sean and I weren't official, we were at least public. And then it became official not too long after that. One night we were at his house, sitting on the couch, when he turned to me and said, "Naya, will you be my girlfriend?" No one had asked me that since elementary school, and I was thrilled. Great, I thought, got a boyfriend now! Check that box off.

I think Sean fell in love very quickly, and it was genuine, even if in retrospect, it seemed like a child falling in love with a new toy. But I was equally swept up in it. He was fancy! He had a big personality and always liked to be at the center of attention wherever he went, so when his attention was on me, it made me feel like, well, at *least* three million bucks. He *sang* to me, and when he rapped about me in a Drake song ("My new girl is on *Glee* and shit / Probably makin' more money than me and shit"), it made me *so* proud, because I felt like he was proud of me. Dudes (if there are any of you reading this book), piece of advice here: being supportive of a woman's career and aspirations is a *guaranteed* way to knock her off her feet.

After six months of dating, we were engaged.

We were in Detroit when he decided to pop the question. I don't think he'd given it much thought. I'd flown out for one of his shows, which was a big deal to him because this was his hometown, so he knew tons of people there, and it was a crowd that had always supported his career. He wanted to blow their minds, but, instead, a whole bunch of technical problems turned the show into a complete disaster.

He was really upset about the whole thing, and I felt bad for him. Back at the hotel, we had a long heart-to-heart, just sitting on the balcony and talking for hours. I tried to be the epitome of a supportive girlfriend that night, as I talked him up and tried to lift his spirits. "Who cares?" I said, and reminded him that it was just one bad show in a string of awesome ones. Overall, he was still doing great.

My pep talk must have worked a little *too well*. Because later that night, when we were in bed and about to fall asleep, he rolled over and nudged me awake. "Hey," he said, "do you want to get married?"

Ummmmmmm, whhhhhhhhhhattttt? I was suddenly no longer sleepy but wide awake and totally incredulous. Was he seriously asking me that, right now? Where was my ring? Where was my *anything*? I thought he was just joking, which I also thought was a totally assholish thing to do, and so we got into a huge fight. I even grabbed my pillow and tried to sleep in the other room. Eventually he sweet-talked me back into bed, and also into agreeing to marry him. *Okay, so we were going to get married.*

Or whatever.

He could be quite the charmer when he wanted to be, but since I still wasn't 100 percent convinced that he was serious, I didn't want to let myself get too excited. The next morning we were having breakfast with all his people and his mom, who I hadn't seen since the steak house colonic discussion. Without consulting me, and in between bites of waffles, he announced to the entire table that we were engaged. "Well, that's not a surprise!" his mom squealed as I spilled my coffee. Just like that, I had a fiancé.

Once we got back to LA, he officially proposed—complete with a private dinner at his house and a drive that ended back at the site of our first date. But the ring was barely sparkling on my finger for a minute before the problems became too big to ignore. For starters, it seemed like he spent more time out of state than in it. I hadn't minded his constant travel or the physical distance all that much before, but now that we were planning a wedding—a wedding that was his idea in the first place—not being able to get a hold of him was more than just an annoyance; it was a serious issue.

Once the wedding became something real, it seemed like he wanted no part of it. I couldn't even get a guest list from him, which was a double pain in the ass because all these rappers had aliases! Like I knew what Wiz's real name was! So there I was, trying to be a grown-up about a grown-up thing and navigate all the practicalities like, Where are we going to live? Are you moving into this house or should I sell this house? Let's get this prenup signed. But I was doing it all on my own, and I might as well have been blasting my texts straight into outer space for all the response I was getting.

I was starting to see that the realities of a relationship just weren't sexy to a rapper who wanted to have his cake and not just eat it too but spread frosting all over the place. (*Too much? Sorry not sorry!*)

Naturally, we started to fight. The more disinterested he acted, the more I'd pull back and try to freeze him out, or just get pissed off, though neither tactic ever seemed to lead to any kind of resolution. Once, we'd been fighting for five straight days while he was traveling, and then on the one day that he was back in LA, he said he didn't want to see me. I was like, "Well, asshole, I've got a key to your house, so I'm just going to come see you."

I walk in, go downstairs, and guess what little girl is sitting cross-legged on the couch listening to music? C'mon, people, I'm not going to tell you, but you can guess because *it's not that hard!* (It rhymes with "Smariana Schmande," if you're really having a hard time.)

Finally, he suggested we go to couples therapy. I wasn't entirely enthusiastic about the idea, because I felt like he'd messed things up and was now trying to get me to help him fix it, but against my better judgment (yes, I know, again) I agreed.

For our first therapy session, he was late. I was sitting there like a truant kid in the principal's office as the therapist kept asking, "Is he lost? Should I call him?" After twenty-five minutes of being alone at couples therapy, he showed up—wearing an all-over weed-print sweatshirt with a giant picture of four asses in thongs on the front. That was the shirt he'd chosen to wear to try and work out our issues? It was so ridiculous that I might have even laughed, had I not been so mad and embarrassed. Also, it wasn't like we could even begin to work out our issues because the session was half over by the time he got there.

The next time, he was prompt, but when I brought up a major issue we'd had, he went ballistic. Listening to his re-action to what I thought was a very valid concern, I almost blacked out; like, I'm supposed to marry this person sitting next to me? Who is this person? The panic rising in my throat, I blurted out: "This isn't going to work! We don't be-long together!"

"Wow," he said. "Do you really feel that way?"

"Yeah," I answered. "Right now I do."

Finally, he was being serious and hearing me out, and af-ter a conversation we decided—together—to postpone the wedding.

But back to that whole him not-dealing-with-real-life thing—when you postpone a wedding, there's money in-volved, and we'd already sent out our save-the-dates. We had to pick out a new time to get married, but before we could, he left town again. Then I was stuck with my mom and wedding planners calling me to ask when the new date was, and all I had to tell them was, "Um, I don't know . . ."

But even with all that, I was still in—amazingly enough. Then the straw that broke the camel's back was a Rolex.

On our third date, he'd given me a Rolex watch, a fancy gift that I'd initially resisted. It wasn't my style, but he pressed it on me, as it was something he'd had for a minute and now wanted to pass on to me. Shortly before everything started to go down in flames, he'd asked me to start wearing it more often, so it was in my regular rotation and I always kept it in the same place. But this time, when I went to look for it, the Rolex was gone. Call it woman's intuition, but I knew immediately what, or who, had happened to it.

In my mind, taking something from someone's house without telling them amounts to theft, even if it is something you gave them. If he'd wanted it back, all he had to do was ask. I was pissed, and it was another WTF moment in this rapidly deteriorating relationship. "Are you stealing things from me now?" I asked when I called him, and he stammered that the only reason he'd taken the watch was to get it rewound. Likely story—people had seen him wearing the watch, and he'd even had it on when he took my brother to a Dodgers game.

In one of my weakest moments OF ALL TIME, I tweeted about it. And, alas, between our millions of combined followers, such a tweet did not go unnoticed—even when I realized what I had done and deleted it as fast as I could. That tweet shall henceforth be known as "The One Time I Showed My Ass on Twitter."

He responded in kind, but in a way, way bigger fashion: he had his publicist release a statement saying the wedding wasn't just postponed, but that he'd decided to call it off. So I learned that I was no longer getting married from THE

INTERNET, and at the same time as the rest of the world. And, not only were we no longer getting married, but apparently we weren't even together anymore.

You know that thing you do in sixth grade where you have your best friend break up with your boyfriend for you? This was like that times a million, and we were adults (well, at least one of us was). It wasn't like your typical celebrity breakup, where a couple releases a joint statement yammering on about "irreconcilable differences." Instead, he did it on his own, and basically said, "Yup, dumped that bitch."

It was sad and beyond hurtful, but at least the relationship had finally come to an end—I didn't love him enough to become a better person, and it was clear that he didn't love me enough to boss up either. As soon as I calmed down enough to take a step back, I could see exactly what had driven our relationship, and why it hadn't worked: we liked the glitz and glam that came with being together more than we actually liked each other. When I heard the word "engagement," I thought marriage, babies, picket fence (albeit a really, *really* fancy picket fence), but I guess he was just thinking PUBLICITY, PUBLICITY, PUBLICITY.

At the time, I didn't really pick up on this, though, because I was so caught up in it. I'd lose track of whose event was whose. When we were going to a party, or had a photo shoot, I didn't know whether the invite had come from my publicist or his. Either way, he got his picture taken and I brushed off the fact that I no longer did anything on my own. I just thought, "Oh, we're a dynamic power couple—of course we're here together."

It became clear to me that a lot of things he did in the name of being "supportive" were really just attempts to share the spotlight. When I had a single drop and it was my turn to do an interview at Power 106, Sean showed up with a bottle of champagne. Just here to support you, babe! But then why are you on the mic? Why are you answering questions about my song?

I guess that's his MO—flash forward to him on the Grammys' red carpet with "Smariana." It was her first time being nominated and now, when she looks back at pictures of that night, he's going to be in all of them. And they're not even together anymore. Just stop. If you're really a supportive man, then you know when to step aside and let your lady be the center of attention. You don't need to literally stand in front of her to prove you were there. You can just as easily make your point from the sidelines.

As soon as my relationship with Sean was over, I recognized that this was a good thing. I think deep down I had always had little twinges of doubt here and there, but, man, do I wish I would have paid attention to them. I would have saved myself a whole lot of trouble.

I DON'T FUCK WITH YOU, EITHER

I've only seen Sean once after he released the statement about how we were no longer getting married. With that, he raised the stakes, and now that I'd seen how bad things could get, I was willing to wave the white flag. I called him and asked him to meet me in person, and we sat on Mulholland, in my car, and talked. I was ready for a truce, and my one request was that he not put my name in shit. Do not write songs about me, I begged, because people are already going to assume you're talking about me, so just downplay it as much as possible. He promised me that he would never do that, and assured me that he was *not* that kind of person.

At this point, I'd heard the beginnings of "I Don't Fuck With You," which was just a beat and a chorus. I actually thought it had the potential to be one of those awesome LA songs that really defines a summer. I was a fan of it, but I had to bring it up.

"Please don't make the lyrics about a relationship."

He was aghast that I would even suggest such a thing. "That song's not even about a relationship," he said. "There are plenty of things people don't fuck with. Some people don't fuck with steak, some people don't fuck with pot roast . . ."

What the hell was he talking about? "Are you kidding?" I asked. It can be about how you don't fuck with kale, just please, please, don't let it have the words "ex" or "girl" in it.

He agreed, 100 percent.

The song dropped a few months later.

"Bitch I don't give a fuck about you or anything that you do / I heard you got a new man, I see you takin' a pic . . ."

What the hell?

Once again, the gossip sites were churning out headlines and my mother was calling me and yelling into the phone,

"Why does that fool's name come up every time I google my kids?"

Dammit—so I was an adult who had dated a child. I learned from that.

And now I have a rap song about me. That's almost as good as a star on the Walk of Fame, right?

THERE IS SUCH A THING AS BAD PR

If there's one thing gossip sites love . . . wait, make that two things they love: one, gossip (duh); and two, kicking a lady when she's down. My newly single self was ripe for both. These sites were reporting that Sean called off the engagement because I was jealous and controlling, and that I had . . . "violent fits of anger"? Let me tell you about the first time I *almost* had a violent fit of anger: when I read that.

Another story had me yelling at him and saying, "If you don't listen to what I say, I'll ruin your career." I mean, who says something like that? No one, that's who. And especially not me.

You know it's time to take the BS seriously when your publicist wants to have a conference call. For a couple of days it seemed like I was on the phone nonstop, but in the end I decided not to release a statement of my own. I was already sick of dealing with it, and I hoped that if I stayed quiet and kept it classy (lesson learned, Twitter), the whole thing would soon blow over. Then Sean and I could both keep it movin' and get on with lives that no longer included each other.

At the same time, I decided I was going to make the best out of my love life suddenly being in shambles, and focus all that extra energy on my career. Keep it professional. Then that also hit the fan. And the gossip pages.

It was the end of *Glee*'s fifth season, and it had been a rough year. Everyone who worked on the show was already stressed. To say that *Glee* means a lot to me is an understatement, and there are a lot of people who worked on that show who I love dearly. Chris Colfer is one of them. He's not only a talented performer, but he's also a bestselling author and just a generally amazing human being. When we were on set, in between takes, he'd be off in a corner, writing novels in longhand in a notebook. I don't know how he did it, but it's incredibly inspiring.

At the producers' request, Chris had written the second-to-last episode of the season. It was a pretty big deal for him, and for the show. The days we shot were crazy, with even more mayhem than usual. Two of Chris's favorite things are animals and old people (see? I told you he's amazing) and he made sure that this episode included plenty of both. There were three-legged dogs running around, and legends like Tim Conway on set.

However, all this caused one particular *Glee* star to amp up her bitch factor. She made a huge deal about the dogs and demanded hand sanitizer any time one came near her. While the rest of us were in hysterics over Tim Conway's constant improvising, it was throwing her off. Instead of just rolling with it, she kept interrupting. "So, like, um . . . are we going to do the scene as it's written now?"

Come on—if Tim Conway wants to improvise, you let him improvise! He'd even brought his granddaughter to the set because she was such a *Glee* fan, and she ended up crying because she couldn't understand why someone was being such a bitch to her grandpa. Finally, my costar gave up, locked herself in her trailer, and refused to come out.

Trust me, I would have been fine with her staying in there (like, maybe forever?), but the sad truth was that we couldn't film without her. People were pulling their hair out and yelling into their walkie-talkies, like, "Can we get her back on set? Can we get her out of her trailer?"

We were shooting a scene in a diner, and all the producers and crew were in a huddle—no one knew what was going on, and absolutely nothing was happening. Meanwhile, one of the producers was just perched on a stool at the counter, like we were in a real diner and he just stopped by for a milkshake!

When I started at *Glee*, the producers told us three things: show up on time, know your lines, and hit your mark. So I listened—I take that kind of stuff seriously, and I know that as much as acting is about performing and having a big personality, it's also about *doing a good job*. I never dropped a line in six years of working on the show. So there I was: I'm on time, I know my lines, and I'm on my mark—and I'm the only one.

I wasn't trying to be Captain Save-a-Hoe, but, as you've probably realized by now, I'm a blunt person. So when things get to a boiling point, like they were that day in the diner full of dogs, I am going to say something. So I walked up to our producer and said, "Are you going to do anything about this?" He looked at me like he had no idea what I was talking about.

"Where are the other people in this scene?" I asked him, gesturing at all the empty chairs around me. "And," I added, "you're on my mark, so if you would kindly get up and handle something—*anything*—that would be awesome."

He lost it, and started screaming at me in front of the crew. "I've been running this show for six years!" he yelled.

Without raising my voice, I responded, "Yes. *Poorly.*"

Ooooh, girl, wrong thing to say, cause after that, Nay Nay didn't get asked back to work.

By the time I woke up the next morning, every gossip site in Hollywood seemed to be cutting and pasting the headline "Naya Rivera Fired from *Glee*." Oh crap. So now, not only did the world know I was dumped, but it also thought I got fired in the same week.

But I hadn't actually gotten fired, not even close. The producer just said he needed a break, and during the summer hiatus, we met and he apologized. I accepted and apologized too—I know now that you're not supposed to tell your boss they're doing a poor job—but I also let him know I didn't think my one comment warranted the smear campaign. I told him that, to be quite honest, I felt like I was under attack.

He insisted they had nothing to do with the rumors, and reading between the lines, it sounded like there was a giant, blinking arrow pointing right at a certain person. So I guess you can throw a bitch fit, lock yourself in your trailer, and stall production, *yet still* allegedly find the time to leak stories to the press. I nodded. Well, I thought, that person doesn't write my lines or write my checks, so I don't give a flying fuck, and we're moving on.

The unexpected silver lining to a really horrible time in your life is that it can actually be somewhat empowering. It makes you realize how much control you do have—not over what is happening, but over how you choose to see it. So I could sit there and be depressed and feel like a victim, or I could pick myself up and get on with it. If I have a personal philosophy, it's "keep it moving," so that's exactly what I did.

FIGURING OUT THE GOD STUFF

The first thing I did to keep it moving was actually to stop. I needed to be with myself and be quiet, and let the storm pass. One of the weirdest things about being an entertainer is that it's a constant push and pull between "Look at me! Look at me!" and "No, don't look at me!" (Picture me passing out on a fainting couch as I wail that last line.) You can get so drunk on fame and all the fanciness of being the center of attention that you forget all the attention doesn't just vanish as soon as you're over it. I was going to have to keep my head high and deal with this mess, and the only way to do so was to detach. I had to forget about my ex, forget about the people on the Internet, forget about my costars. I had to just be with myself, and with God.

For two weeks, I barely left the house. Now, I don't want this to sound sad, like I was curled up in bed in dirty sweatpants, stuffing my face with Doritos—I still took the time to brush my hair, but I also just took some time to reflect. There's a difference between keeping it movin' and just doing things to distract yourself; I knew that running myself ragged wouldn't help me move in a productive way. It'd just leave me burned out or totally crazy, and I'd just end up looking like Amanda Bynes on a bad day. Physically, she *walks around a lot*, but she does not keep it movin'. Poor girl. The last thing I wanted to do was party it up and give the tabloids something else to sink their teeth into.

I also took advantage of this time to start to pray a lot and to go to church. I really think that whoever you are, and whatever you believe in, you need to find something that gets you to a calmer place and makes you feel refreshed. It's edifying. For some people that thing is yoga, or reading self-help or philosophy books, but for me it's church. I'm Christian and grew up going to church, and the principles of Christianity have always resonated with me.

When I was growing up, my mom and dad had very different views on religion, and I respect both of them. My mom became a devout Christian when I was about seven; she started to watch the Trinity Broadcasting Network and refused to let my brother and I listen to secular music. When I would perform at school talent shows, I could only sing Christian songs (which, let's be honest, didn't really bring the house down at a public junior high).

My dad had been raised a Jehovah's Witness but had no desire to continue down that path as an adult. He had looked into Buddhism for a while, and frequently meditated, but on the whole he wasn't a fan of organized religion. Whenever he saw my mom loading us into the car on a Sunday morning, he liked to point out to us kids that we didn't have to just automatically assume we were Christians, and that there were other things out there. So file religion under "Another Thing That Drove a Wedge Between My Parents."

I completely understand where my dad was coming from. Religion and spirituality should be about your personal relationship with God. But for me, I didn't need to look around or search for anything, because Christianity had felt right from the beginning. Going to church felt good, what I learned there made sense, and I felt a real connection to God. Whenever I go to church, or pray, I feel refreshed, and afterward, the whole world seems a lot clearer.

By the time I was a teenager, my mom had loosened the leash a little bit, and going to church was no longer something she was going to force us to do. But I still always found my way back to it. Whenever I would realize that I wasn't praying and wasn't reading the Bible anymore, it felt like I was dropping my relationship with God. I would always notice that when I started to do this, things also stopped working out, or I didn't feel right in a way that I couldn't quite put my finger on.

The year 2014 was a wake-up call—for the past two years, everything had moved at the speed of light, and they were going so well that I forgot they could get bad. Whenever there is commotion and noise in my life, I go back to the Bible and my relationship with God, and that steers me where I need to go. I think that's pretty typical for a lot of people, and it takes something bad to remind us that connecting with our spirituality and our own inner strength is something we should be doing on a consistent, not just as-needed, basis. When I prayed, I made it a point to say, "Thank you for this time, because I know that something good is going to come out of it, and I know that I need to calm down right now."

I didn't want to pray like this: "Things are so bad—get me out of it!" I wanted to be grateful, because taking things for granted is a great way to turn yourself into a lazy bitch. When you get to that point, you stop appreciating the things you do have and quit working for the things you don't.

For me, the words "be still in the Lord" ring very true. When I talk to God now, I try to strip away all the problems and anxieties that I want resolved and instead focus on the bigger underlying issues. Like, what decisions did I make that led me to this place? I never ask for God to fix things for me, or to make things go away, only to give me guidance so I can become a better person and fix them myself.

I do believe that God has a plan for everyone, and that our lives our predetermined. So if I believed that God was steering my ship, why was I always trying to steer everyone else's? I had to learn how to trust and to mind my own business at the same time. God has a plan, and even if I think that plan is really shitty at first, I have to trust that it will all work out in the end.

In this case, it did. And even better than I could have imagined.

I LOVE A GOOD ELOPEMENT

It was during this time that Ryan came back into my life. He'd seen the headlines and heard the gossip, and sent me an e-mail: "Hey, I heard about all this stuff, and it seems pretty shitty. I was a fan of his music before you guys were together! I just want to make sure you're okay, so let me know if you want to talk."

As with everything that happened with Ryan, the timing was eerily perfect. The day before, my sister had been at my house as I was randomly Insta-stalking him: "He was always so nice! Why don't you date him again?" So when his e-mail landed in my inbox, I looked up his phone number, called him, and asked if he wanted to meet up. He did, and it was that night that I told him about the abortion. When he slept over, I remember being really nervous, and climbing into bed wearing a hoodie that he zipped up to my neck. I turned my back to him and just went to sleep. I didn't want us to just hook up and then have that be that. I felt like I'd just crawled through the fire, and getting burned had taught me that I was ready for something real. Ryan was real.

Shortly after, he left to shoot a movie in Albuquerque. I went out to visit him, and that was when we fell crazy in love. It was one of the best times of my life. I went to the set with him one day, and just sat there and watched him work— it felt so nice to be on the sidelines and watch someone else work—especially someone who is as passionate about what he does as Ryan is.

Albuquerque, New Mexico, is a lot like Valencia, California—there's a BJ's and a Chili's and a Target and not much else. We went to all those places, shopping for snacks or eating fried artichokes and having a blast. We once spent hours just reading magazines and looking at books in a Barnes & Noble, then bought booze at the local liquor store and just hung out in his hotel room. No one knew who we were, which was a relief.

I flew back to LA, and before I knew it, I'd planned another trip back to see Ryan. The night I returned to Albuquerque, we sat in BJ's, our new favorite restaurant, for hours, just talking about serious life stuff: marriage, kids, what we'd seen our parents do and what we'd learned from that. What we wanted for ourselves. Jokingly, I asked, "So, are we getting married?" but he answered me seriously.

"Well," he said, "I don't know . . ." Which was not a "no." We continued to talk about it, and when I was back in Los Angeles, he called me one night. "Let's do this. We're getting married." Hell yes.

The next day, I had lunch with my mom. "So how was Albuquerque?" she asked.

"It was good," I said. "So I think we're going to have a wedding in Mexico?"

Now, mind you, my mom at this point had been hearing Ryan's name for four years but had never actually met him. I half-expected her to reach across the table and slap me.

Instead, she was thrilled. "Oh my God," she squealed. "Naya, that's so perfect!" Like I said before, my mom has had my back through plenty of ups and downs, but she went on to tell me that since Ryan and I had started dating again, I'd seemed calmer and more secure than she'd ever seen me before. He treated me well, and it brought out my best qualities. With him, she thought, I acted my age, not my shoe size. Mom was all for it.

After that, Ryan and I fast-tracked and met each other's families. No matter how weirded out they were, they all came. My stepdad told me that he didn't think it was really going to happen, but that if it did, he would be there. My brother took some convincing, because he thought we were crazy, but in the end he walked me down the sand aisle.

We got married at Las Ventanas, a beautiful resort in Cabo. After all the press I'd been through with my previous breakup, I worked extra hard to make sure the wedding wasn't going to be covered by the media until I was good and ready for it. We told the resort that the ceremony was a vow renewal for my mother and her husband, which worked out great—except they write the bride's and groom's names in the sand. A representative kept calling and asking, "What's your mom's name?" and I'd always find a way to put them off. "Um, I'll just give you the names when I get there, okay?"

JUST BECAUSE YOU DON'T KNOW ABOUT SOMETHING DOESN'T MEAN IT'S A SECRET

All our caution paid off—no one crashed the wedding, and it didn't hit the press until we announced it. All the gossip sites acted like put-out babies because they hadn't known about

© DINO GOMEZ PHOTOGRAPHY 2016

it in advance. The headlines called it a "surprise" or "secret" that "came out of nowhere." They suggested that I'd kept the same wedding and just swapped out the groom, which truly is #triflin.

Sean and I were supposed to get married in Santa Barbara, not Mexico, and Ryan and I didn't get married on the same date—we got married on Ryan's birthday. I had bought a Carolina Herrera dress for my wedding with Sean and wore

Monique Lhuillier when I married Ryan. (Still trying to sell that Carolina Herrera dress, actually. DM me on Twitter if you're interested. Good price, I promise.)

What's more—just because we didn't send TMZ an engraved invitation doesn't mean we were keeping it a secret. Everyone who mattered to us knew about it in advance, and many of them were there to be part of it.

And it definitely didn't come out of nowhere. The truth was quite the opposite—it was really four years in the making, and next to when my son was born, it was the best day of my life.

2014 didn't turn out so bad after all.

SORRY:

- *Falling in love with the idea of a person, instead of the actual person.*

- *Ignoring my intuition and staying in a relationship that I knew deep down wasn't right.*

- *Putting someone on blast in a public way rather than talking about it one-on-one (a.k.a. showing my ass on Twitter).*

- *Getting snappy with my boss instead of just taking a deep breath and deciding to STFU.*

NOT SORRY:

- *About that broken-off engagement. Best thing that ever happened to me.*

- *Praying with gratitude as opposed to just asking God to make the bad stuff go away.*

- *Trusting that every shit storm has a silver lining.*

- *Taking responsibility for my actions and apologizing to my boss.*

- *Planning a "secret" wedding that included all the people we cared about. And only those people.*

- *Laughing at the gossip instead of getting upset by it (same wedding dress, my ass).*

WHAT ARE YOU?
Finding the Beauty in Being an "Other"

T FIRST STARTED to dawn on me that race, and my race especially, was a complicated issue when I started to do Cabbage Patch doll commercials as a kid. I'd look around and see that the white girl was holding a blond doll, the Asian girl had an Asian doll, and I had the black doll.

When I'd bring this up to my mom later, she'd say, "You know, back in the day, if you had a drop of black in you, then you were black." And that made sense—I guess—and I started to realize that because my mom was half-black, to white America, I was black, or at least black enough.

But really, I'm an "other."

My dad is half–Puerto Rican and half-German. His father, George senior, was born in Puerto Rico, and his mom, Anna, was born in Yugoslavia. Family rumors surrounding Anna abound—one of them being that her family's farmland was taken during World War II, landing her in a working concentration camp, but somehow she managed to bust out. One of her legs was shorter than the other, so she always wore a boot (this is not a rumor, but fact). Her family was very racist, and after she married George, they never spoke to her again.

My grandfather only spoke Spanish and my grandmother only spoke German, so who the hell knows how they communicated. They met in an ESL class, so maybe there was enough broken English between the two of them to get by. My dad and his brother spoke almost exclusively German, as well, until he was old enough to go to school. George senior was a Jehovah's Witness but also a heavy drinker. When he'd had too much, which was often, he'd come home, take out his gun, and start shooting shit, or try to light the house on fire. Anna committed suicide when my dad was just nineteen years old. To say he'd had an unhappy childhood is a gross understatement, so immediately after his mother's funeral he drove cross-country, to California, and never looked back.

My mom, Yolanda, was born in Chicago to a fourteen-year-old black mother and an eighteen-year-old Puerto Rican dad. As a baby, my mom was anemic and sickly, and since her mom's parents didn't want to keep a mixed grand-baby, she was placed in foster care.

She went to a home where several other foster kids were staying with a woman who was already in her forties. One by one, all the other kids were adopted or returned home to their biological parents, until my mom was the only one left. She was considered a ward of the state until she was eight years old, when she was legally adopted by her foster mom, and shortly thereafter they moved to Milwaukee.

My mom didn't know she was adopted until she was a teenager, when she found a letter from an adoption agency in the attic. Her adoptive mother and sister were black, and as my mom was dark skinned, she had grown up thinking she was purely African American. When she confronted my grandma about the adoption, Grandma denied it, and my mom decided not to push. She figured that Grandma had given her a really good life, and if she didn't want to talk about it, then that was her right. Mom never brought it up again. To this day I view Grandma as a saint and know that, had she not adopted my mom, I wouldn't be here.

So cue 50 Cent here, because my parents met in da club. My dad was ten years older than my mom and had already been in California for more than a decade when he went to Milwaukee to visit his brother. They went out, and saw my mom and her best friend, Tracy, who's white and still my mom's best friend to this day.

Dad's brother saw the two girls standing there—Mom was nineteen, six feet tall, and gorgeous, so hard to ignore—and asked, "Do you want the black one or the white one?"

"I'll take the black one," Dad said.

And boom. The rest was history.

If my parents had issues as a mixed-race couple, we didn't hear about it. A lot of their friends were also in interracial relationships, and in California in the 1990s they didn't face the same kind of discrimination that their parents had. But I knew I was an "other," and exactly what kind of other, before I knew my address or my telephone number. At auditions, my mom would fill out the forms with all my basic information, and when it came to the question of race, she'd always check the "other" box, and then write out exactly what I was: one-quarter African American, one-quarter German, and one-half Puerto Rican (from two different sides of the family, no less). Mom made sure to instill my racial identity in me, as well. "People are always going to ask my kids what they are," she said. "And it's important that they know."

And Mom was right—to this day, I still get the "What are you?" question all the time—from reporters in interviews to people I work with to friends of friends I meet at a party. I'm always tempted to answer, "I'm fucking human," but instead I give them the answer they're looking for. The worst part is that after someone's asked you this question, and you've answered it, there's really no place else to go with this conversation. They'll usually follow up with something like, "Oooh, so exotic!" or "Quite the mix!" like I'm a puggle. I always think I should start going up to white people and asking them, "So, what are you?"

People always ask me what Ryan is, and I just laugh—he's all the whites with a drop of Cherokee in there somewhere. We're a biracial couple, and our son is half–all the whites, one-quarter Puerto Rican, one-eighth German, and one-eighth black.

I'd like to believe that my children will have a better go of it than I did, but who knows? I'm still shocked by the number of mean tweets we get: "I can't believe he's with that whatever-she-is" or "What's up with Naya got her a white guy to try to be white." And people will @ us in these racist tweets!

I guess that in 2016 people are just as racist and crazy as ever.

NOT FITTING IN—ANYWHERE

While I may have been black enough for Mattel, it wasn't that clear-cut once I got to school. I soon started realizing that I was too white for the black kids, too black for the Latinos, and just generally too all-around other for the white kids.

From an early age, most of my friends were white just by default, as my whole school and most of our community was white. When I played Dorothy in the elementary school production of *The Wizard of Oz*, one of the only other nonwhite students in the school—a black girl named Christina—also got cast in the play.

As Toto. All she did throughout the play was follow me around, and her only lines were to occasionally bark: "Woof, woof!"

I remember my mom being pissed after the performance, though I was too young to completely understand why. "Oh hell no!" she said, slamming a drawer in the kitchen. "I wouldn't let my black daughter be the dog at this white school."

Still, though, my mom could turn on the white like a party trick. No doubt that, in Valencia, it was a survival skill. At home she'd yell at us kids like, "Not up in my house, you don't!" But then when she'd run into a neighbor on our cul-de-sac, her speech would be dripping with Waspishness. "Oh hi, Noelle," she'd coo. "How are you?"

If we tried to call her out on it, she'd always deny it—"I don't talk white!"—and act like we were crazy.

I picked up techniques, and which race I hung out with wasn't so much about who I identified with the most but who would take me. By junior high, I was trying to be as white as possible because that was what needed to happen in order to avoid spending my lunch breaks alone.

My brother, on the other hand, who was only four years younger than me, identified with black culture from an early age. He's darker skinned, with features more like my mom's, so he looks more African American than mixed. He also played football and went to schools where there were tons of other black kids, so it was easier for him to get in where he fit in.

Our high school quad was an exercise in segregation. The KKK would have been proud, because there was no race mixing. One day at lunch, I was standing near the black kids when two of the girls called me over.

"Hey," they said. "You were in that B2K video, weren't you?" It was an in, and I was taking it.

"Oh yeah!" I said. "I'll tell you anything you want to know. Anybody want their phone numbers?"

They squealed in excitement. "Sit down and tell us everything! We love them. We love Raz-B. Ooh, you're cute. You got great hair!"

This was my first time really having black friends, and I felt like my eyes were opened to so many things. It even helped me get over my eating disorder, as they were always pointing out that I was too skinny and that guys really liked thick girls. No matter who I was hanging out with, though, it wasn't long before someone pointed out to me that I wasn't totally with my people. There was another girl we hung out with who was half-Asian and half-black, and my new friends didn't think twice about making sure neither of us forgot that we weren't "full black." Eventually it turned into something of a joke. I'd try to laugh it off, but really I just felt like I couldn't fully be myself with anyone.

It often felt worse with the white kids, though—maybe that was just because there were more of them. Someone was always holding their arm up to mine and talking about how much darker my skin was than theirs, and yet people wouldn't think twice about calling someone a nigger in front of me. I never knew how to react. Like, was I that great of an actress that now all these fools really did think I was white? Did they not see me standing here? Did they not know my mom is half-black?

I wasn't scared to call people out in the moment, and point out that what they'd just said was racist and offensive, but as soon as the dust settled, I'd be terrified that I'd overstepped my bounds. What if I'd totally outed myself as someone who was definitively not like them? What if that was the first step to not having any friends? When you feel like you can't stand up for yourself, that's pretty fucked up.

I remember once in high school, two of my girlfriends

(both white) and I drove down to Hermosa Beach with three white guys from our school. We were sitting at a gas station, when one of the guys told a joke. It was something stupid that didn't even really make sense—like, "What does a nigger say to a parrot?"—but it was also obviously offensive.

I blacked out with anger and started yelling at him. "Are you really that ignorant that you think something like that is funny?" I asked. "Because I'm not laughing."

He apologized, but it had totally killed the mood. Except nobody seemed to think it was his fault for telling a racist joke in the first place. Rather, it was mine for reacting to it. As soon as us girls were alone, one of them sighed. "That really wasn't a big deal," she said. "You shouldn't have gotten so worked up about it." And with that, I was the other once again, and an outcast for the rest of the trip.

IT'S A HAIR THING

Even if I'd just been mute every time one of my white friends made a racist comment, I still wouldn't have totally fit in. My hair blew my cover.

I didn't have classic African American "nappy" curls, but I still had curls, and lots of them. Whenever I'd do shoots as a kid, the stylist would always ooh and aah over my hair and tell me how great it was, but I hated every strand of it. As soon as I was old enough to compare myself to the other girls in my class, I wanted straight hair, but Mom wasn't having it (probably because she knew how much work it was).

So instead, I went to extreme measures to try to tame my mane.

My days started each morning at six, when my alarm would go off and I'd get up and take a shower. I washed my hair every day, because I needed it to be thoroughly wet, and the only time I could get a comb through it was in the shower when it was slicked with conditioner.

As soon as I got out of the shower, and when my hair was still soaking wet, I'd drench it with gel. At this point in the nineties, the scrunch look was in—super grateful for that, because I could rock the scrunch look. I couldn't do any re-scrunching throughout the day, though, because each lock of hair was so crispy with gel that it just bent in half.

I shopped for hair products in the ethnic and white aisles at Target. I was down to use whatever worked, and I wanted it all. I used Pink Oil Moisturizer Hair Lotion, which is a classic ethnic hair product, and since I used so much of it, I'd buy the cheapest gel I could find.

I also tried to use all the products my best friend, Madison, was using, figuring that maybe if I used white-girl products, my hair would come out looking white. No dice on that, though. Bed Head After Party Smoothing Cream sure did smell great, but didn't do shit on my hair.

Whatever product concoction I was using, though, I always made sure to finish it off with a heavy layer of Aqua Net Extra Super Hold hair spray. If there is a hole in the ozone directly above Valencia, California, it's probably my fault.

On days when I'd oversleep, or somehow didn't have the energy for all the upkeep, I'd just slick it back into a bun.

Either way, my hair was always sopping wet when I left for school in the morning, because I wanted to make sure that I was frizz-free for as long as freaking possible. My shirt had a constant ring of water down the back, and on particularly cold mornings I was freezing.

My life would have been so much easier if I'd just carried my product arsenal with me, but for some reason I never thought of that. Instead, I just dreaded PE with every ounce of my being. PE ruined everything.

On picture day, in sixth grade, my mom had actually made my hair look really cute. It was down and curly but not so voluminous that it completely took over. But then—the horror and the injustice—my time slot to get the photo taken was right after PE!

I was having a meltdown in the locker room, because an hour of dodgeball had rendered me a frizz ball, when my friend Kelti offered to help. "My sister's half-black," she said. "I know how to do this." I instantly trusted anyone with a biracial sister.

She marched me over to the sink and just dunked my whole head under the faucet. As soon as my hair was sopping, she twisted it up into a wet bun. In the photos, it didn't look that bad, but it didn't really look that good either. It just looked wet. Still, I was eternally grateful to Kelti for showing me the way, and after that, I dunked my own head every day after PE.

The day of my junior high graduation was the first time my mom let me straighten my hair, and she even did it for me. At this point, we were well into the twenty-first century and hair straighteners had been around for at least a couple of decades, but somehow this news hadn't made its way to my mom. Instead, she went about as old school as you could get, using a hot comb that she had to heat up on the stove each time before she raked it through my hair. The whole process took hours, and I was stiff at the end of it from trying to hold super still to make sure I didn't get burned.

Soon after, my mom bought me a real straightening iron so I didn't have to use the hot comb anymore, and every night I wrapped my newly straightened locks up in a scarf and put a bonnet over my head, like I was a 1960s-era southern housewife.

This was a trick I'd learned from Tia and Tamera Mowry. We'd gone to their house one day after church, and they were barely in the front door before they'd wrapped their hair. I'd never seen anyone do that before, and they explained to me that this was how they kept their straightened hair soft and silky.

This was when Tia and Tamera were on *Sister, Sister*, and they'd just gotten a joint Lexus for their eighteenth birthday. I thought they were the shit, and if they were wrapping their hair, then I was going to do it too. "Mom," I said as soon as we left, "buy me clips!" After that, whenever I wasn't out in public, my hair was wrapped.

With the straightening, the parting, the clipping, and everything else that went along with my new straight-hair lifestyle, plus my extensive journaling and list making, my nights were booked solid. It's amazing I found the time to not eat.

Now that I'm pushing thirty, I don't have to do anything to my hair anymore. And, no, this is not a good thing—it's just that after three decades of fighting with your hair, it gives up. My hair may blow out easily now, but it's also thin, and I wish I could get back the amount of hair I used to have, even if that hair was super curly.

I felt the same way about my hair as a lot of mixed and black women do. A lot of us have complicated feelings about what grows out of our head, and I think that's because, deep down, most of us have been conditioned to try to blend, pass, or fit in. White people are always trying to tell ethnic women what they should and shouldn't do with their hair—here's how you "tame" those "unmanageable" curls; or here are "professional" hairstyles, a.k.a. styles that look the most white.

Even if there were a couple of ethnic Cabbage Patch Kids, most "other" little girls grow up being constantly exposed to blond-haired, blue-eyed women as the ideal of beauty. We know we can never look like that, so eventually we start to interpret that to mean that we can never be beautiful either. It's an identity issue passed off as a bad hair day.

It cracks me up that having a weave used to be something that only "ghetto" black women did, as if it was some kind of shameful shortcut. Now every white girl I know is running around with hair glued to her head.

And my hair may be straight now, but I am never without extensions. They're how I get my powers and where I keep my secrets.

My extensions will never tell.

BLACK-AND-WHITE ISSUES

My family has never been very PC. When we're together, we represent blacks, whites, and Latinos, and that makes us feel like we could say whatever we want. However, when I'm not with my family, it's hard to take a lighthearted approach to talking about race. I learned this firsthand when I cohosted *The View* and made a comment about how showering daily is such a white-people thing. I said this because my husband showers a lot.

The words were barely out of my mouth before people were up in arms about it. Some people thought it was racist against white people; some people thought it was racist against minorities because it implied that they were dirty. I apologized, and was truly sorry to have offended anyone, because that wasn't my intention. The backlash from my offhand comment drove home just how hard it is to talk about race, especially when you're biracial. I love a good "white people be like" joke, but I guess people think I'm too white, or maybe not white enough, to make them. Never mind that I've been called the N-word to my face more than once. Sigh. You can't win.

That's also the case with a lot of castings—a lot of the entertainment industry sees race as such a black-and-white issue, which can be pretty limiting when you don't fit entirely into either category.

I think of the nineties, when I was a kid, as the golden era of black sitcoms—when a lot of shows like *Family Matters* or *The Fresh Prince* were family comedies with black casts.

They weren't necessarily about being black. There also weren't a ton of Latino roles in those days, so it was very natural for me to be cast as a black girl.

Now it seems like there's a lot less leeway in the roles that are written for nonwhite characters, in that race will inevitably play a big part in how they act and what they say. During a recent pilot season, it seemed like there were a bunch of new black shows in development. I had the opportunity to audition for one of them, playing the wife of a well-known black comedian. As soon as I got the script, though, I knew this wasn't the part for me, as every other line was something about being a sista. Coming out of my mouth, it would not have worked.

I called and explained this to my agent. He agreed, and called the casting director to see if there was any leeway. He called me back a few minutes later. "They said, 'We don't care how much black she has in her. She just has to have some.'" That, right there, was enough for me, and I didn't go to the audition.

At this point in my career, I've been acting for more than twenty years. You would think that, over the course of two decades, I'd have witnessed industry stereotypes and racial prejudice evaporate, but unfortunately, that doesn't seem to be the case. My race is just as big a deal in 2016 as it was in 1996, and I recently had a white executive tell me that the size of my lips was "too distracting" for the role I wanted to play.

That kind of comment is so stupid that it should just make me laugh—and it does, in a small way—but it's still hurtful. It's hard to think that I did a better job than some white girl, but that she's probably still going to get the part for reasons that are entirely outside of my control. Shouldn't we have moved past that by now?

The sad truth is that a lot of the roles that are available for black or Latino actors are stereotypes. They're not nuanced, three-dimensional characters; they're black guys who have only white friends but still call everyone "my brotha." Whenever I see a role like this, I'm reminded that somewhere there's a white executive who shoehorned a few nonwhite characters in last minute, because they didn't want to get fired for not having any diversity on the network that quarter. And that sucks.

Granted, there is more diversity on TV now than ever before, but I still look forward to the day when black and Latino and Asian and all us "others" actors can just be, you know, *actors.*

Wouldn't that be swell.

SORRY:

- *Being so mean to my hair that it decided to leave me. Come back, come back!*

- *That I wore a wet T-shirt to school basically every day of junior high. It sounds sexy, but, yeah, it wasn't.*

- *Offending anyone with my comments on* The View. *I know it's hard enough out there for people of color, and I don't want to make anything worse.*

- *That actors are still typecast based on their races. Twenty-first century, people—let's get with it!*

- *Racist Twitter trolls. I'd tell you to fuck off, but you're not worth my time.*

NOT SORRY:

- *About being an other.*

- *For sticking up for every part of myself, even if it was just the one-quarter that was black.*

- *For rocking the shit out of my scrunched hair.*

- *For never fitting into one particular group of friends, and therefore getting a taste of different cultures.*

BFFS, BAD GIRLS, BITCHES, AND MY MOM
Learning to Love the Ladies

DON'T HAVE A ton of friends, and I never have. I don't have a gaggle of girlfriends that I go everywhere with, I don't wake up to forty-seven new messages in a group text every morning, and I don't have standing girls' nights where we drink wine and talk shit on everyone we know.

And you know why? Because I like it that way.

When it comes to friends, I'll take quality over quantity any day.

I met Madison, one of my best friends and partner in crime, in second grade. I honestly don't remember how we met, because positive classroom memories from that year are completely overshadowed by our creep of a teacher, Mr. Bonterra, who once plucked an eyelash off my cheek and then held it out in front of me on his finger and said, "Blow." So, so not appropriate.

Madison is white—and blond-haired gorgeous white at that—and her family had more money than mine, but at that age those differences paled in comparison to bigger second-grade issues, like our aversion to people who ate gross food for lunch or who picked their nose.

However, I do remember going over to Madison's house after school. She lived in a suburb with a man-made lake and paddleboats, and she had all the American Girl dolls, accessories included! Still, I wasn't jealous; I was just stoked to get to play with that kind of doll at all.

Even though Madison and I didn't always go to the same school, we were always close, and by high school we were inseparable. We called each other Scoobs—we still do to this day actually—and I'd talk to her several times a day on my pink Motorola Razr (I liked the sound it made when it snapped shut) or on my Swarovski-crystal-studded Sidekick phone that she customized for me during her bejewel-everything phase.

We kept a notebook—our version of a *Mean Girls* slam book, though we were never that mean. We passed it back and forth all through high school. We'd write each other letters during class or at home in the middle of the night when we couldn't sleep. She'd write notes to hype me up when I was applying for a job at Red Robin, and then write another note consoling me when I didn't get it. (C'mon, Red Robin! Your restaurant is not that hot!)

We filled the notebook with drawings and doodles of our summer plans (laying out on beach towels) or where we saw ourselves in ten years. We drew stick figures of ourselves

The notebook Madison and I shared in high school—she's been my partner in crime since day one.

with word bubbles coming out of our mouths. Hers said, "The name is M. Hees, interior decorator to the stars!" and mine said, "I'll take two Bentleys, please!"

In that notebook, we spent a lot, and I mean *a lot*, of time writing and drawing pictures about how much we loved Jamba Juice.

The one time in my life that I snuck out of my parents' house was with Madison. We were living in that shitty apartment by the railroad tracks, but Madison had come over to spend the night. We were doing what we always did in those days, which was watching and rewatching *The Notebook*.

That was when there was that weird trend where everyone was painting their house keys—why?—and I had painstakingly coated mine with pink nail polish with green polka dots. Madison was flipping through magazines and wouldn't stop talking about how she wanted bangs.

Finally, after an hour of this, I was like, "Fine, I'll cut your bangs!" but then I couldn't find any scissors. Madison was so excited that she suggested we just go to CVS and get some, even though it was eleven thirty at night and my parents were already asleep. I was nervous, but Madison had a car and insisted everything would be fine.

I shut my bedroom door and left *The Notebook* playing, so if either of my parents did get up, they'd assume we were still in there. Then we crept out of the house, and I shut and locked the door behind me as quietly as I could.

We went to CVS, got the scissors, and made it home without incident. Then, when I went to use my brand-new pink-with-green-dots key to unlock the door, it was so thick from being coated with nail polish that it wouldn't fit in the hole. We spent the next half hour trying to scrape the paint off it on the side of the door, and by the time we finally whittled it down and got back in it was already after one.

Madison still wanted bangs though, so in my bedroom I made up a makeshift beauty salon, complete with lamps and a towel over her shoulders. Then I proceeded to give her the worst haircut she's ever had in her entire life.

The next morning, we came out of my room to my mom yelling, "Naya, do you know anything about that pink shit scraped all over the door . . . ?" She trailed off as we walked into the kitchen and she caught sight of Madison's horrible bangs, which hadn't been there the night before. They looked like they'd been cut with pinking shears, and the right side was distinctly shorter than the left. She spent the next six months growing them out, but as proof of how good a friend Madison is, she wasn't even mad about it.

When I was in elementary school, the other kids all thought it was cool that I was an actor, but in high school it just made me even more of an outcast. Without even talking to me, people just assumed that I was stuck up, so they'd ignore me or even go out of their way to make sure I knew they weren't impressed.

Madison never made a big deal about it, though. She never judged me for any of it, and cared in exactly the way I needed a friend to care as a teenager. She'd check in—"Hey, how'd that audition thing go? Did you get the job?"—and then when I'd tell her that I didn't and I didn't want to talk about it either, we'd move on and she wouldn't bring it up again.

Once I booked *Glee* and my acting career started to take off, she didn't change. She never pressed me for industry gossip or asked me what celebrities were like in real life. Even when my ex started to very publicly date someone new, Madison acted like she couldn't care less. And she didn't just act like she didn't care—she really didn't. Every once in a while, she'll see a photo shoot and text me, "Scoobs, you look so pretty!" but that's about it. And always Scoobs, never Naya.

Madison and I have definitely had our ups and downs, as is to be expected when you've been friends with someone for two decades. The people you love will always get on your nerves in little ways, or there will be things you don't agree on, but one of the best things about getting older is that all of a sudden these kinds of things become easier to brush off. You're not screaming, "Why are you trying to ruin my life?" at someone just because she was fifteen minutes late picking you up to go to Target.

Madison and I are so ingrained in each other's lives that I can't imagine mine without her. When we go out now, I always offer to pick up the check. Not because that is what she expects—she would never do that—but because this is the girl who bought me makeup, gave me rides, visited me at Hooters, and even helped me put cat food on a dude's car. I owe her big, and dinner is the least I can do.

THE WORST BEST FRIEND

Just because I had one great friend didn't mean that I didn't also make some super shitty ones here and there. My parents still remember my worst best friend, even though I'm almost thirty and it was more than ten years ago. Every once in a while, something will remind my mom of it, and she'll say, "Well, nothing could be as bad as when you were hanging out with that Angie . . ."

I met Angie at the ground zero of shitty decisions—Hooters. Angie was the aforementioned ex–pageant girl from Texas whose mom tried to teach me how to do my own extensions. (Maybe that was karma for what I did to Madison's bangs?)

I don't think the nature of our friendship was all that unusual. A lot of girls have that one best friend for a while, who you bond with—not because you can trust each other or have a lot in common, but because you're bored and want someone to go out with. Fortunately, these friendships don't last long.

I met Angie when I was probably at my lowest point ever. I'd all but given up on acting, given up on everything, and was falling back on the only asset I thought I had: my looks. When I met her, I thought we were just meant to be friends: she had fake tits (just like me!), her mom also lived in Valencia (just like mine!), and she had lip injections (I didn't but thought it was so chic . . .).

As soon as I got to Hooters, it skeeved me out that I was using my body to make money—even if it was just in the name of hot wings and fried pickles—and I think that was what attracted me to Angie in the first place. Unlike me, she had no problem with men looking at her like she was just a piece of ass. On the contrary, she even seemed proud of it, and her bravado was almost awe inspiring. ("Almost" being the key word here.)

Angie was all about getting whatever she could out of whomever she could, and never felt guilty about it. After she got her lips done, she and her mom flew to New York to make an appearance on a talk show about teenagers with plastic surgery. "I think it's totally fine!" her mom said, smiling into the camera.

Angie also believed that if a guy offered you money, you took it. And if a guy didn't offer you money, well, then that was when you asked for it. She seemed to have about a dozen sugar daddies, ranging in age from just a few years older to a few decades older. "Yeah, but do you do anything with these guys?" I'd always ask. She would answer in a way that made it impossible to tell if she'd just said yes or no.

She lived in a decent apartment with her parents and drove a decent car they paid for, so if I ever wondered what she needed all the money for, I had my question answered the first night we went out: all that sugar-daddy money went straight up her nose. Usually we went to Hollywood clubs where we could slide past the velvet (velour?) ropes with our fake hair and even faker IDs, but sometimes Angie would call me up to go "party" and it would turn out to be just four or five people sitting in a disheveled living room doing drugs.

One such evening, Angie did line after line of cocaine off a coffee table until the sun was starting to come up. She was my ride, so I was basically as good as trapped and sat there sipping on vodka tonics until I drank myself sober again. Mind you, I was no angel, and had definitely tried drugs myself a few times, but it was never the main event. I was finally able to convince her to leave, and she drove me home, her teeth grinding the whole way.

The next day was Angie's birthday, and she'd planned a big party for herself at the pool in her apartment complex— she'd swindled one of her many male ATMs into giving her four hundred dollars to buy supplies. The next morning, even though it felt like I'd only been asleep for an hour, she came and dragged me out of bed to go shopping with her.

She bought throw pillows at IKEA to furnish the pool house, tons of booze, decorations, and snacks. Her mom made a cupcake tree, and she sent out the invite to more than fifty people. As the party time rolled around, and then passed, it became more and more obvious that the only guests coming were me and the guy who wanted to check on the return on his investment.

I was so hungover, I felt like scratching my eyes out, and finally the combined headache and awkwardness of the situation wore on me, and I bowed out early to go home and take a nap.

A few hours later, Angie called and woke me up for the second time that day, and demanded that I come meet her at Universal CityWalk for dinner. I agreed—because it was her birthday and I felt bad that no one came to her party—but when I met her, she was in a fouler mood than I could have anticipated. In the brief period of time since I'd seen her,

she'd gone and gotten her septum pierced, and then proceeded to accuse me of making her do drugs and ruining her
life. I took one look at her new face jewelry, a full bull ring
in her nose, and knew right then and there that this friendship had run its course.

I have no idea where Angie is now. After that day, I
stopped answering her texts and phone calls, and it wasn't
long after then that I quit Hooters and started to get my
own shit together. When I think back on it, I feel sorry for
her—her life clearly sucked. She'd moved to Los Angeles
with her crazy family and was convinced that she was going to make it big in Hollywood, but the closest she got to
that dream was a self-made entry into Oprah's search for
the next great talk show host. I obviously didn't feel that
great about myself either, so we were a pretty unstable
combination. You can't be a good friend to someone else
unless you're a good friend to yourself first, so neither one
of us contributed anything more than drama to that
relationship.

Never feel bad about cutting someone out of your life—
sometimes that's the only option. When you hang out with
people who are true friends, you come away feeling lighter,
more inspired to work hard, give love, and take care of yourself. When I hung out with Angie, I always felt totally
drained afterward, like I needed a green juice and some
Deepak Chopra to get my body and mind right. I wasn't myself with her and I'm glad I finally recognized that.

When you're deciding whom to be friends with and
whom to let into your life, you have to look for quality peo-

ple who bring out the best in you, the kind of people you can stay in and watch *The Notebook* with, the people who will still hug you even when you have snot running down your face because you've just spent the last two hours crying about some asshole who cheated on you. And then you have to do the same for them. A friendship is just as much give-and-take and compromise as a romantic relationship, so you will get out what you put in.

Don't take your friendship cues from *The Real Housewives* and build relationships off superficial things you have in common, like money or the same plastic surgeon. It's also too easy to get caught up in wanting to be friends with the coolest girls, the ones who seem to know all the guys and can get into all the clubs, or the ones who will look hot in your Instagram photos (#brunchwithmybitches). But beware. If you choose your friends based only on what you think they can do for you, someday you're gonna find yourself brunching alone.

FROM ONE BITCH TO ANOTHER . . .

When it was announced that I was writing a book, everyone expected me to use it to rip Lea a new one, so let me list just a few of the reasons why I'm not going to do that: one, I have better things to write about; two, it doesn't bring you up to bring someone else down; and three, I don't hate Lea, and I never have.

One of the *Glee* writers once said that Lea and I were like two sides of the same battery, and that about sums us up. We are both strong-willed and competitive—not just with each other but with everyone—and that's not a good mixture. When two people with strong personalities are friends, or in any kind of relationship, they're eventually going to clash. And maybe they'll get over it; maybe they won't. Lea and I didn't.

In the beginning, Lea and I were friends on set and off. We always had a good time together, and it seemed like we were building a friendship. We'd go to the spa together, or she'd go pick up takeout from Real Food Daily and then we'd just sit around at her house. We were the kind of friends who didn't have to make specific plans; we could just hang out. I remember once going over to her house and sitting on the bed while she cleaned out her closet, giving my opinion on whether I thought she should keep or toss articles of clothing (or, you know, give them to me).

Once, shortly after Lea and Cory started dating, I told her she needed to slut it up a bit. And instead of slapping me, like one might have expected her to do in this situation, she agreed. I went and picked her up at her house, and we went shopping at Kiki de Montparnasse—it was a very Santana and Rachel outing. I helped her pick out all this sexy lingerie, and told her that her body looked great, and then we went and ate sandwiches and drank beers afterward.

Cory called in the middle of it, and when she answered, she laughed, "I just went lingerie shopping and now I'm eating a sub. I must be hanging out with Naya."

As the show progressed, though, that friendship started to break down, especially as Santana moved from a background character to one with bigger plot lines and more screen time. I think Rachel—erm, I mean *Lea*—didn't like sharing the spotlight. On top of that, she had a hard time separating work from our outside friendship, whereas it was a lot easier for me. I'm not offended when people offer feedback or criticism, and if things get heated on set, I try to keep perspective. We're all stressed, yes, but we're all working toward the same goal, so laugh it off and keep it movin'.

Lea was a lot more sensitive, though, and sometimes it seemed like she blamed me for anything and everything that went wrong. If I'd complained about anyone or anything, she'd assumed I was bitching about her. Soon she started to ignore me, and eventually it got to the point where she didn't say a word to me for all of season six.

Lea and I definitely weren't the best of friends, and I doubt we'll ever sit on her couch and eat kale together again, but the rumors of our "feud" were blown out of proportion. Whenever anything good would happen for either her or me—when I got married, or when she started dating someone new—there would always be stories quoting anonymous sources that just swore up and down that we were still trashing and mocking each other. I never did that. I'd like to think that we both have better ways to spend our time, but as Santana and Rachel proved on *Glee*, a bitch fight, even a made-up one, does make for riveting drama.

In the end, I do wish that Lea and I had gotten along better, but I'm not losing sleep over it. I don't trust people who claim to like everyone, because, really, how is that possible? If that is true, then you must not have any standards. If you care about your life, then there are going to be certain people you don't want in it.

I also don't think you can worry too much about it when someone doesn't like you. I'm not saying you should never pay attention when people call you on your shit, but if you are committed to being your honest and authentic self, then you are going to piss a few people off here and there. You just have to learn how to not take it too personally, and definitely don't obsess over it. It comes back to the idea of gratitude and being thankful for what you do have instead of focusing on what you don't. So instead of worrying about who doesn't like you, take some time to remember who does. And then go call them. Now.

SPELLING "LOVE" M-O-M

By this point in the book, you've probably already guessed that my mom and I are close. Well, the truth is that we're closer than close. Ryan says he's never seen anyone talk to their mom as much as I do. We talk at least three times a day, usually on FaceTime. I call her as soon as I find out something good, or something bad, whenever I'm excited, or whenever I panic (like the time when I was pregnant and thought I found a stretchmark on my boob. It was FaceTime, so she basically answered a call from my tit).

Mom's my ultimate number one, and I'm hers. We're best friends, family, and drinking partners. When I got pregnant with Josey, she was obviously super excited, but after a few

Me and my mom, two ride-or-die chicks.

months she was bored—with me off the sauce, she claimed there wasn't anyone who would drink martinis and talk shit with her.

As much as you can talk to your friends about what is going on in your life, I think it's important to have someone who has more perspective. For me, that's my mom. I always go to her for advice, and I trust her to tell me the truth—be it good or bad. She hasn't had the easiest life, but I've never heard her complain. She's one tough lady, and I'd like to think she passed that on to me. It's probably because I am so much like her that we did fight so hard core when I was in high school.

That, and hormones. When I try to think about why so many teenage girls go through a period of hating their mom,

I think it has got to be hormones that make us stand at the top of the stairs and scream, "You don't understand me! I wish I'd never been born!" before storming off into our room and slamming the door.

From the moms' point of view, it has got to be hard to have to look at your daughters and say, "I don't understand why you're not getting it. I told you—I did that, and it turned out horribly, and you're still going to do it?"

If I ever have a daughter, at least I'll be able to literally throw this book at her and scream, "Oh yeah, I don't understand?! Well, you can just read about all the shit that I did!"

Love you, Mom . . .

SORRY:

- *Everything about my bad-girls-club stint with Angie, and all the head-splitting hangovers that went with it.*

- *Trying to base a friendship on superficial qualities.*

- *That everything between Lea and me got so blown out of proportion.*

- *All those times I scrawled "I HATE MY MOM" in my journal.*

NOT SORRY:

- *That I have a few amazing friends instead of a bunch of so-so ones.*

- *That I dropped Angie. Sometimes you have to cut people out of your life and not look back.*

- *That I don't always get along with everyone. Having people not like you is a risk you have to take to be real, and I'll take that over being fake any day.*

- *That my mom is a badass who's always got my back. With her in my corner, I can do anything.*

10

SORRY NOT SORRY

EVERYONE SHOULD WRITE a book.

No, I'm serious.

Break out your journal, open up a Word doc, grab a crayon—whatever it takes, do it now. When you set about putting your experiences down on paper—all the good stuff, the bad stuff, the times you got fucked over, and the times you fucked up—this amazing thing starts to happen.

You begin to have a whole new perspective.

You start to connect the dots.

You see that what you always regarded as a string of random events isn't random at all.

Instead, it's your life.

When I started writing this book, I knew I didn't want it to be the kind of book everyone expected me to write, which was a trashy tell-all that talked a whole bunch of shit—I'll write that book when I am eighty-five and just don't give a fuck anymore. And even though as a teenager I stood in line at the Valencia Walmart to buy the Paris Hilton book (and get it signed), I didn't want it to be that kind of book either—one filled with glamorous photos to illustrate the "perfect" celeb lifestyle.

I wanted to write a book that was real. One that was inspiring and that shed some light on the fact that growing up is hard, and that, contrary to what people try to tell you all the time, there is no such thing as a perfect life. We're probably our most perfect right when we come out of our moms' vag, but we just get more and more imperfect from there on out. That's what makes us human—that we screw up, make bad decisions, and take wrong turns. We can only hope to learn from all of them, and maybe, if we're lucky, laugh a little bit.

When I say "sorry not sorry," I'm saying that I don't regret any of the things that have happened in my life, and I attribute that directly to my relationship with God. Even in my worst moments, I had to trust that God had a plan for me. I might make mistakes, but He doesn't.

I remind myself of that every day. I may be sorry that I did certain things and sorry about the consequences that I faced because of them. I may say sorry because I owe someone an apology, but I'm definitely not sorry that everything happened the way it did. I wouldn't take any of it back, because if I did, then I wouldn't be where I am now, and I wouldn't have any good stories to tell. So when life gives me lemons, I say fuck it and drink champagne.

I always meditate on the idea of love, and I always want to be a source of love. God is love, and God is in everything, therefore everything can be love. I want to share that in whatever way I can, whether that's being a source of light or happiness or even—especially in 2014—just a distraction. I hope that with this book, I can give a little love to someone who might recognize herself in these pages, and maybe that love will help her feel a little less alone.

I also think a lot about what it means to love yourself. Everyone is always telling you to love yourself, though no one ever tells you how to go about doing it. Learning how to love yourself is something everyone struggles with. I know that I wasn't loving myself when I would go an entire day refusing to eat even an apple, or when I would go club-hopping in Hollywood rather than face up to the fact that I wasn't doing anything productive with my life.

I love myself now—I'm happy with my career and have an incredible husband and a child that I love more than anything in the whole wide world. But even now, it's hard. There's still a thirteen-year-old girl inside me making detailed lists of how I can improve, who's never sure of my own self-worth.

When I'm always moving full-speed ahead and thinking about what's coming next, it's hard to take a step back and say, "Naya, I love you," but that's what I'm trying to do now. After I had the abortion, I didn't think I'd ever forgive myself, and if I'm being honest, I'm still not sure that I have. But I am closer than I ever have been before, and even if I can't ever totally move past it, I am at least aiming for forgive and never forget.

I knew that I never wanted to have children until I could provide for them in a way that made us all comfortable, because I didn't want them to have to go through what I did growing up. I wanted to own a house. I wanted to be with someone who possessed the qualities I admire in a guy: talent, kindness, a sense of humor, ambition (and, okay, really hot). When I take a step back, it blows my mind that I was able to achieve these things. I still have so much further to go, but, still, I feel successful already.

Success isn't limited to money, awards, your dress size, or how long your IMDb page is. Success can be anything you want it to be—whether it relates to your career, your personal life, or the little things you want to do on a daily basis. If all you want to do on a given afternoon is get froyo—get it, and that's success. Success is not defined by what the people around you want. It is based on what you want for yourself. People often lose sight of the truth that everyone has a different path toward success—it's easy to fall into a hole of constantly comparing yourself to others. That's a great way to sap your happiness and turn into an ungrateful bitch. "I only have three Prada bags and she has four! My life is the worst." You don't want to be that girl.

As funny as I now find my crazy junior high to-do lists, I am proud that I kept them. List making gives you a concrete and visual reference for what you want for yourself, much like a vision board does, and that's important. It holds you accountable and can help get you back on track when you start to stray. Being ballsy enough to bullet-point your future gives you confidence, and this is the first step toward having the future you want. If you don't have some way of checking in with yourself, you're always just going to be bouncing around like a pinball, losing your direction and going whatever way seems to be the easiest.

I think I was born motivated and with my eyes on the prize, but I also don't understand what the other options are.

Being lazy, not doing anything with your life, settling for less than your best, dwelling on every little thing that goes wrong—that is not the way to live. If that offends you, well, sorry—not sorry.

xo,

Naya

ACKNOWLEDGMENTS

To my mother—you're the love of my life and one ride-or-die chick. Thank you for everything.

To my Ryan—you're a close second. ;-) Thank you for knowing exactly who I was from day one and always being all about it.

To my Josey—thank you for being the best part of my story and choosing me to be a part of yours.

To my family and friends, for countless late night talks, guidance, distractions, and love.

To everyone who made my dreams of being an author come true: Kate Williams for helping me shape these pages. Joanna, Sara, Lauren, Eric, Justin, UTA, Inkwell, and TarcherPerigee.

Lastly, to everyone I've ever liked, loathed, loved, kissed, bad-mouthed, slept with, dumped, hung out with, worked next to, or befriended. Without you, my story wouldn't be what it is today. Thank you.